Portús na hÉireann

Portús na hÉireann

A Book of Hours according to the Columbanian Tradition

Dustin A. Ashley

RESOURCE *Publications* · Eugene, Oregon

PORTÚS NA HÉIREANN
A Book of Hours according to the Columbanian Tradition

Resource Publications
An Imprint of Wipf and Stock Publishers
199 W. 8th Ave., Suite 3
Eugene, OR 97401

www.wipfandstock.com

PAPERBACK ISBN: 978-1-6667-3827-8
HARDCOVER ISBN: 978-1-6667-9876-0
EBOOK ISBN: 978-1-6667-9877-7

03/23/22

To the pious Christians of Ireland, Scotland, Manx, and their descendants in diaspora, who have lost their ancestral faith or have kept their traditions alive despite adversity.

A Thighearna, dèan tròcair oirnn.

Contents

Acknowledgments

This book is a project that has taken years of long nights and arduous labor to bring into fruition. If it wasn't for my amazing support group, namely my professors, colleagues, friends, and family, then this project would have been another idea to emerge and be quickly forgotten.

I should start by thanking my mother, Carrie Ashley. As I began my path into seminary and this endeavor, she offered continuous encouragement and helped me nurture this idea into its current form. I love you, Mom.

I wish to thank the professors at Emmanuel Christian Seminary, specifically Dr. Rollin Ramsaran, Dr. Paul M. Blowers, and Dr. Gary Selby, who offered key insights and advice on developing this text. Through regular conversations, the academic and liturgical quality of this book was greatly improved.

I thank the Matthew Wimer, the editor at Wipf and Stock, who has been a great help in making this book accessible to all interested in the liturgical practices of the early Irish church.

Introduction

Within the history of the Christian Tradition, the beliefs and unique culture of the Church is modeled on the principle of syncretism. As a synthesis of Jewish and Greco-Roman culture, Christianity exists as a purifying force that appropriates and adapts the best aspects of both. While the Early Irish tradition is known for their nature-oriented theology and their zeal for asceticism, its liturgy proves to be one of the most obscure subjects within Christian history. As the indigenous liturgical practices were overturned by Carolingian reforms, there are no later sources that provide clues as to how Irish liturgy was celebrated. Academics have turned to sources outside of the few manuscripts, most notably the Antiphonary of Bangor and the Stowe Missal, investigating Irish literature. Stories, such as the *Navigatio sancti Brendani*, provide clues as to how Irish monks worshipped. The interpretations of these texts by academics have yielded a more comprehensive view as to how an Irish breviary was possibly celebrated, acknowledging the degree of liturgical variety present within the Early Irish Church.[1]

The *Portús na hÉireann* is a liturgical book that contains the texts of the Divine Office, the most exalted form of prayer in Christianity second only to the Divine Liturgy. Translated as "Irish Breviary," the title is an Irish derivation of the Latin *breviarium* meaning abridgement, signifying its concise form for the purpose of lay worship. The contents of this book are an amalgamation of prayers and hymns from the *Navigatio sancti Brendani*, Antiphonary of Bangor, and the Stowe Missal. As these texts are attributed to St. Columbanus, an Irish monk from the seventh century, this book is a representation of the Divine Office as was celebrated within the Columbanian tradition.[2] The *Portús* allows Christians to worship in a traditional

---

1. While the purpose of this text is to faithfully replicate an 8th century mode of worship, it does not attempt to become the authoritative version. The Early Irish Church is known for its liturgical diversity, as noted by St. Columbanus in his *Regula Monachorum*.

2. The liturgical hours presented herein are admittingly derived from the Columbanian tradition, albeit with the Gallican influences. See Jeffery, "Eastern and Western

manner, consistent with how Early Irish monks would worship throughout the day. This method teaches individuals to pray carefully, examining our hearts and minds as we use our breath to glorify his Holy Name. Reciting the prayers contained therein provides the opportunity for Christians to connect with the spirituality and *ethos* of the Early Irish Church, participating in Christ as it was known to them.

Liturgy of Hours

The *Portús* is composed of eight liturgical hours, consisting of psalms, gospel readings, and various collects to be chanted during when specified. The first set of hours, known as the minor hours, are referred to as Seconde, Terce, Sext, and None. These liturgical hours are celebrated during the hours of 6 a.m., 9 a.m., noon, and 3 p.m. respectively. The day hours are short, composed of three psalms per hour and a hymn of one's choice. As the day hours are primarily spent working, times for prayer meant individuals would pray individually in their own cells. The second set of hours, known as the major hours, are referred to as Vespers, Duodecima, Nocturn, and Matins.[3] These hours are celebrated during the hours of 6 p.m., 9 p.m., 12 a.m., and 3 a.m. respectively. The night hours are much longer, composed of twelve psalms and hymns corresponding to each hour. While the day hours are for private worship, the night hours are designated for corporate worship.

The Divine Office is a Christianized version of the Jewish practice of praying at fixed hours, known as *Shacharit* (morning prayer), *Mincha* (afternoon prayer), and *Maariv* (evening prayer). This practice was continued within the Early Christian community where they followed the Apostles in praying at the third, sixth, ninth hours of the day, and at midnight.[4] Hippolytus gave instructions to pray seven times per day in the *Apostolic Tradition*, drawing influence from Psalm 119:164. The canonical seven hours was brought to Gaul through the *Institutes* and *Conferences* of St. John Cassian, outlining his experiences with the Coptic monastic communities. His texts eventually came under the possession

---

Elements," 118.

3. Seconde, Duodecima, and Nocturn correspond with Prime, Compline, and the Night Vigil respectively. These designations are derived from St. Cassian and are used in the Antiphonary of Bangor. See Warren, *The Antiphonary of Bangor*, xvi.

4. Acts 10:3; 16:25

of Irish monks, where St. Columbanus adapted Cassian's works and established the eight canonical hours in his *Regula Monachorum*. This pro-
duced a unique Divine Office within Western Christianity that was highly
influenced by Coptic monastic worship.

Structure

Each hour consists of an invitatory, psalm selection, hymn, gospel read-
ing, and a series of prayers that terminate with the Divine Prayer and a
moment of silence. The invitatory is a series of prayers that begin the Office, beginning with the prayer "God, make speed to save us; Lord, make
haste to help us"[5] and the Minor Doxology. These, and the remaining
prayers, are the most consistent part of the hour and serve as an invitation
to come and worship.

   Psalmody within the Divine Office serves as the focal point of worship, to which most of the material consists of individual psalms. This was
intended by monastics as a means of 'praying without ceasing,'[6] a tradition
brought to the West through the influence of Sts. Jerome and Cassian.
To the Irish monastics, psalmody was given great affection to which they
could not conceive of a Christian life without the canonical praises of
God. This profound love for the psalms is present in the poetry of Máel
Ísu Ua Brollcháin, indicating a deep contemplation of psalmody's role in
monastic and Christian life.[7]

   The psalm selection, or *cursus psalmorum*, is derived from the *Navigatio sancti Brendani*, a work of fiction understood to be allegorical by
academics.[8] This *cursus psalmorum*, consisting of three psalms attributed
to the minor hours and twelve to the major hours, is a combination of the
Palestinian and Coptic traditions and illustrates a strong influence from
St. Cassian. While the text fails to provide a rubric for every night Office,
it offers a selection for each minor hour, Vespers, and Matins.[9] The *cursus
psalmorum* is given as follows:

5. Psalm 70:1
6. Luke 18:1
7. See McNamara, *Psalms*, 360.
8. See O'Laughlin, "The Monastic Liturgy," 113.
9. To make up for the lack of psalms for the remaining hours, the psalms for Duodecima and Nocturn were derived from the Coptic *Agpeya*.

1. The Night Office (*ad uigilias matutinas*)

   Ps. 148

   Ps. 149

   Ps. 150

   12 additional psalms 'in the order of the psalter'[10]

   A concluding collect

2. Prime

   Ps. 50

   Ps. 62

   Ps. 89

   A concluding collect

3. Terce

   Ps. 46

   Ps. 53

   Ps. 114

   A concluding collect

4. Sext

   Ps. 66

   Ps. 69

   Ps. 115

   A concluding collect

5. None

   Ps. 129

   Ps. 132

   Ps. 147

   A concluding collect

10. This has been interpreted to mean the complete psalter was read in groups of 12 over several days, which has been adapted as 'sessions' in the Order of Matins. See Jeffery, "Eastern and Western Elements," 109.

6. Vespers

Ps. 64

Ps. 103

Ps. 112

The 15 'gradual' psalms seated i.e., Pss. 119-133[11]

As each hour exists to commemorate Christ's passion, death, descent, and resurrection, the *cursus psalmorum*, hymns, and gospel readings were carefully chosen to correspond with the hour's theme. Collects and versicles are said at different liturgical hours, and at the end of psalms and hymns. Derived from the Antiphonary of Bangor, they are said according to Eastern and Western practice that was present in the Columbanian tradition but was not adopted into the Roman Breviary.[12]

Suggestions for Lay Worship

While the length of this text may be daunting to lay members, it is important to remember this is a book of prayer. When praying in accordance with this book, the duration should be only to the extent that one can endure. Do not push yourself to pray beyond your mental or physical limitations, as the quality of time is more important than the quantity. As stated by St. Columbanus, "So although the length of standing or singing may be varied, a person will achieve equal perfection in prayer of the heart and continual attention to God."[13]

As the desire to pray at each hour is an appealing endeavor, this may not be practical for those with daily responsibilities. When your responsibilities dictate that you can't pray early in the morning, during the day, or late at night, focus on the times when prayer is possible. It is more important to pray when you can, rather than force yourself to pray when you can't. In other words, "the realization of this one ideal should be variously valued, for the demands of work and place must be taken into account."[14]

Therefore, one should take this into consideration when developing a consistent prayer regimen. When time allows for one to pray, pray

11. See O'Laughlin, "The Monastic Liturgy," 122–123.
12. See Jeffery, "Eastern and Western Elements," 113.
13. See Kardong, *St. Columban*, 62.
14. See Kardong, *St. Columban*, 62.

ceaselessly. Take a few minutes to examine your heart and mental state, repenting for any transgressions, and prostrating before our Lord Jesus Christ. This will aid in obtaining the spirit of prayer. When a psalm is too long or cumbersome to recite, break it up into ten verses and recite each section at a time. When verbal prayer becomes tiresome, prostrate between each psalm. When you complete a liturgical hour, pause for a moment of silence, and reflect upon the recited words as your own. This will help increase your love and fervor to worship and magnify his Holy Name.

The Order of Matins

Invitatory

God, make speed to save us. LORD, make haste to help us.

Glory to the Father, and to the Son, and to the Holy Spirit, now and ever, and unto the ages of ages. Amen.

Hasten, O LORD, to free us from all our sins; for you live and reign with the eternal living Father and the Holy Spirit, now and ever, and unto the ages of ages. Amen.

We have sinned, O LORD, we have sinned, spare us our sins, and save us; you who guided Noah over the flood waves, hear us; who with your word recalled Jonah from the abyss; deliver us; who stretched forth your hand to Peter as he sank, help us, O Christ. Son of God, you accomplished marvelous things of the LORD with our fathers, be favorable in our days also; Stretch forth your hand from on high.

For Sundays and Easter

Saint Mary, pray for us.

Saint Peter, pray for us.

Saint Paul, pray for us.

Saint Andrew, pray for us.

Saint James, pray for us.

Saint Bartholomew, pray for us.

Saint Thomas, pray for us.

Saint Matthew, pray for us.

Saint James, pray for us.

Saint Madianus, pray for us.

Saint Mark, pray for us.

Saint Luke, pray for us.

All the Holy Saints, pray for us.

Deliver us, O Christ. Hear us, O Christ. Hear us, O Christ. Hear us, O Lord have mercy.

Son of God, you who did marvelous things of the LORD with our fathers, be favorable in our days also; Stretch forth your hand from on high. Deliver us, O Christ. Hear us, O Christ.

A Collect for the Hour of Matins

O God, help us all
Who praises you as Three
And confesses to You as One
With sacred hymns;
Who reigns now and ever,
And unto the ages of ages. Amen.

Another

You are, O LORD, the illuminator of darkness, creator of the elements, and forgiver of sins. Your mercy, O LORD, is great upon those who seek you with so much heart. May your majesty, O Lord, hear us in the morning, and blot out our sins which are not hidden from you, who reigns with you and the Holy Spirit, now and ever, and unto the ages of ages. Amen.

Sundays

An Antiphon Before Cantemus Domino

Moses looked to the right and left,

Led the people in the royal way

Bringing them towards the seashore.

Another

Let us sing to the LORD and magnify his glory.

Cantemus Domino

Exodus 15:1–6, 11–13, 17–18

Let us sing to the LORD: for he is gloriously magnified, the horse and the rider he hath thrown into the sea.

The LORD is my strength and my praise, and he is become salvation to me: he is my God and I will glorify him: the God of my father, and I will exalt him.

The LORD is as a man of war, Almighty is his name.

Pharao's chariots and his army he hath cast into the sea: his chosen captains are drowned in the Red Sea.

The depths have covered them, they are sunk to the bottom like a stone.

Thy right hand, O LORD, is magnified in strength: thy right hand, O LORD, hath slain the enemy.

Who is like to thee, among the strong, O LORD? who is like to thee, glorious in holiness, terrible and praiseworthy, doing wonders?

Thou stretchedst forth thy hand, and the earth swallowed them.

In thy mercy thou hast been a leader to the people which thou hast redeemed: and in thy strength thou hast carried them to thy holy habitation.

Thou shalt bring them in, and plant them in the mountain of thy inheritance, in thy most firm habitation which thou hast made, O LORD; thy sanctuary, O LORD, which thy hands have established.

The LORD shall reign forever and ever.

A Collect after Cantemus Domino

By drowning the Pharoah in the sea, Israel was set free. Through the baptism of grace and triumph of the cross, we pray to be freed from all evil through you, O Christ, who reigns with the Father and the Holy Spirit, now and ever, and unto the ages of ages. Amen.

Another

O Christ God, supporter and protector in the salvation of your people Israel, you led them away on dry earth through the sea. Save us from the yoke of our sins, who reigns with the Father and the Holy Spirit, now and ever, and unto the ages of ages. Amen.

An Antiphon before Benedicite

Three boys begged you

Shouting to you from the midst of the fire

From one voice they sang a hymn.

Another

Utter a hymn, and exalt him above all forever.

Benedicite

Song of the Three Young Men, 35-65

O all ye Works of the LORD, bless ye the LORD: praise him, and magnify him forever.

O ye Angels of the LORD, bless ye the LORD: praise him, and magnify him forever.

O ye Heavens, bless ye the LORD: praise him, and magnify him forever.

O ye Waters that be above the Firmament, bless ye the LORD: praise him, and magnify him forever.

O all ye Powers of the LORD, bless ye the LORD: praise him, and magnify him forever.

O ye Sun and Moon, bless ye the LORD: praise him, and magnify him forever.

O ye Stars of Heaven, bless ye the LORD: praise him, and magnify him forever.

O ye Showers and Dew, bless ye the LORD: praise him, and magnify him forever.

O ye Winds of God, bless ye the LORD: praise him, and magnify him forever.

O ye Fire and Heat, bless ye the LORD: praise him, and magnify him forever.

O ye Winter and Summer, bless ye the LORD: praise him, and magnify him forever.

O ye Dews and Frosts, bless ye the LORD: praise him, and magnify him forever.

O ye Frost and Cold, bless ye the LORD: praise him, and magnify him forever.

O ye Ice and Snow, bless ye the LORD: praise him, and magnify him forever.

O ye Nights and Days, bless ye the LORD: praise him, and magnify him forever.

O ye Light and Darkness, bless ye the LORD: praise him, and magnify him forever.

O ye Lightnings and Clouds, bless ye the LORD: praise him, and magnify him forever.

O let the Earth bless the LORD: yea, let it praise him, and magnify him forever.

O ye Mountains and Hills, bless ye the LORD: praise him, and magnify him forever.

O all ye Green Things upon the Earth, bless ye the LORD: praise him, and magnify him forever.

O ye Wells, bless ye the LORD: praise him, and magnify him forever.

O ye Seas and Floods, bless ye the LORD: praise him, and magnify him forever.

O ye Whales, and all that move in the Waters, bless ye the LORD: praise him, and magnify him forever.

O all ye Fowls of the Air, bless ye the LORD: praise him, and magnify him forever.

O all ye Beasts and Cattle, bless ye the LORD: praise him, and magnify him forever.

O ye Children of Men, bless ye the LORD: praise him, and magnify him forever.

O let Israel bless the LORD: praise him and magnify him forever.

O ye Priests of the LORD, bless ye the LORD: praise him, and magnify him forever.

O ye Servants of the LORD, bless ye the LORD: praise him, and magnify him forever.

O ye Spirits and Souls of the Righteous, bless ye the LORD: praise him, and magnify him forever.

O ye holy and humble Men of heart, bless ye the LORD: praise him, and magnify him forever.

Amen.

A Collect After Benedicite

Hear our prayers, almighty God, and grant that as we sing the blessed hymn of the young men, in your service, we are absolved from the snares of sins and may not be burned with eternal fire, Savior of the World who reigns with the Father and the Holy Spirit, now and ever, and unto the ages of ages. Amen.

Another

You alone, almighty God, we praise your law. As you spared the three young men from the fire, through your mercy deliver us from the punishment of eternal death, who reigns with the Father and the Holy Spirit, now and ever, and unto the ages of ages. Amen.

148

Laudate Dominum

Praise ye the LORD from the heavens: praise ye him in the high places. Praise ye him, all his angels: praise ye him, all his hosts. Praise ye him, O sun and moon: praise him, all ye stars and light. Praise him, ye heavens of heavens: and let all the waters that are above the heavens. Praise the name of the LORD. For he spoke, and they were made: he commanded, and they were created. He hath established them forever, and for ages of ages: he hath made a decree, and it shall not pass away. Praise the LORD from the earth, ye dragons, and all ye deeps: Fire, hail, snow, ice, stormy winds which fulfill his word: Mountains and all hills, fruitful trees and all cedars: Beasts and all cattle: serpents and feathered fowls: Kings of the earth and all people: princes and all judges of the earth: Young men and maidens: let the old with the younger, praise the name of the LORD: For his name alone is exalted. The praise of him is above heaven and earth: and he hath exalted the horn of his people. A hymn to all his saints: to the children of Israel, a people approaching to him. Alleluia.

149

Cantate Domino

Sing ye to the LORD a new canticle: let his praise be in the church of the saints. Let Israel rejoice in him that made him: and let the children of Sion be joyful in their king. Let them praise his name in choir: let them sing to him with the timbrel and the psaltery. For the LORD is well pleased with his people: and he will exalt the meek unto salvation. The saints shall rejoice in glory: they shall be joyful in their beds. The high praise of God shall be in their mouth: and two-edged swords in their hands: To execute vengeance upon the nations, chastisements among the people: To bind their kings with fetters, and their nobles with manacles of iron. To execute upon them the judgment that is written: this glory is to all his saints. Alleluia.

150

Laudate Domino

Praise ye the LORD in his holy places: praise ye him in the firmament of his power. Praise ye him for his mighty acts: praise ye him according to the multitude of his greatness. Praise him with sound of trumpet: praise him with psaltery and harp. Praise him with timbrel and choir: praise him with strings and organs. Praise him on high sounding cymbals: praise him on cymbals of joy: let every spirit praise the LORD. Alleluia.

A Collect for After the Laudate Psalms

We praise you, O LORD, and with your saints, we ask that you support us as you hear our prayers; who reigns with the Father and the Holy Spirit, now and ever, and unto the ages of ages. Amen.

Another

O LORD, God of all souls, we adore you and pray that we may endure safely through this solemn vigil, just as darkness turns into light and the sun shines at noon. Savior of the World, who reigns with the Father and the Holy Spirit, now and ever, and unto the ages of ages. Amen.

First Session

1

Beatus Vir

Blessed is the man who hath not walked in the counsel of the ungodly, nor stood in the way of sinners, nor sat in the chair of pestilence. But his will is in the law of the LORD, and on his law he shall meditate day and night. And he shall be like a tree which is planted near the running waters, which shall bring forth its fruit, in due season. And his leaf shall not fall off: and all whatsoever he shall do shall prosper. Not so the wicked, not so: but like the dust, which the wind driveth from the face of the earth. Therefore the wicked shall not rise again in judgment: nor sinners in the council of the just. For the LORD knoweth the way of the just: and the way of the wicked shall perish.

2

Quare fremuerunt

Why have the Gentiles raged, and the people devised vain things? The kings of the earth stood up, and the princes met together, against the LORD and against his Christ. Let us break their bonds asunder: and let us cast away their yoke from us. He that dwelleth in heaven shall laugh at them: and the LORD shall deride them. Then shall he speak to them in his anger, and trouble them in his rage. But I am appointed king by him over Sion his holy mountain, preaching his commandment. The LORD hath said to me: Thou art my son, this day have I begotten thee. Ask of me, and I will give thee the Gentiles for thy inheritance, and the utmost parts of the earth for thy possession. Thou shalt rule them with a rod of iron, and shalt break them in pieces like a potter's vessel. And now, O ye kings, understand: receive instruction, you that judge the earth. Serve ye the LORD with fear: and rejoice unto him with trembling. Embrace discipline, lest at any time the LORD be angry, and you perish from the just way. When his wrath shall be kindled in a short time, blessed are all they that trust in him.

3

Domine, quid multiplicati.

The psalm of David when he fled from the face of his son Absalom. Why, O LORD, are they multiplied that afflict me? many are they who rise up against me. Many say to my soul: There is no salvation for him in his God. But thou, O LORD art my protector, my glory, and the lifter up of my head. I have cried to the LORD with my voice: and he hath heard me from his holy hill. I have slept and taken my rest: and I have risen up, because the LORD hath protected me. I will not fear thousands of the people, surrounding me: arise, O LORD; save me, O my God. For thou hast struck all them who are my adversaries without cause: thou hast broken the teeth of sinners. Salvation is of the LORD: and thy blessing is upon thy people.

4

Cum invocarem

When I called upon him, the God of my justice heard me: when I was in distress, thou hast enlarged me. Have mercy on me: and hear my prayer. O ye sons of men, how long will you be dull of heart? why do you love vanity, and seek after lying? Know ye also that the LORD hath made his holy one wonderful: the LORD will hear me when I shall cry unto him. Be angry, and sin not: the things you say in your hearts, be sorry for them upon your beds. Offer up the sacrifice of justice, and trust in the LORD: many say, Who sheweth us good things? The light of thy countenance, O LORD, is signed upon us: thou hast given gladness in my heart. By the fruit of their corn, their wine and oil, they are multiplied. In peace in the selfsame I will sleep, and I will rest: For thou, O LORD, singularly hast settled me in hope.

5

Verba mea auribus

Give ear, O LORD, to my words, understand my cry. Hearken to the voice of my prayer, O my King and my God. For to thee will I pray: O LORD, in the morning thou shalt hear my voice. In the morning I will stand before thee and will see: because thou art not a God that willest iniquity. Neither shall the wicked dwell near thee: nor shall the unjust abide before thy eyes. Thou hatest all the workers of iniquity: Thou wilt destroy all that speak a lie. The bloody and the deceitful man the LORD will abhor. But as for me in the multitude of thy mercy, I will come into thy house; I will worship towards thy holy temple, in thy fear. Conduct me, O LORD, in thy justice: because of my enemies, direct my way in thy sight. For there is no truth in their mouth; their heart is vain. Their throat is an open sepulchre: they dealt deceitfully with their tongues: judge them, O God. Let them fall from their devices: according to the multitude of their wickedness cast them out: for they have provoked thee, O LORD. But let all them be glad that hope in thee: they shall rejoice forever, and thou shalt dwell in them. And all they that love thy name shall glory in thee: For thou wilt bless the just. O LORD, thou hast crowned us, as with a shield of thy good will.

6

Domine, ne in furore

O LORD, rebuke me not in thy indignation, nor chastise me in thy wrath. Have mercy on me, O LORD, for I am weak: heal me, O LORD, for my bones are troubled. And my soul is troubled exceedingly: but thou, O LORD, how long? Turn to me, O LORD, and deliver my soul: O save me for thy mercy's sake. For there is no one in death, that is mindful of thee: and who shall confess to thee in hell? I have laboured in my groanings, every night I will wash my bed: I will water my couch with my tears. My eye is troubled through indignation: I have grown old amongst all my enemies. Depart from me, all ye workers of iniquity: for the LORD hath heard the voice of my weeping. The LORD hath heard my supplication: the LORD hath received my prayer. Let all my enemies be ashamed, and be very much troubled: let them be turned back, and be ashamed very speedily.

7

Domine, Deus meus.

O LORD my God, in thee have I put my trust: save me from all them that persecute me, and deliver me. Lest at any time he seize upon my soul like a lion, while there is no one to redeem me, nor to save. O LORD my God, if I have done this thing, if there be iniquity in my hands: If I have rendered to them that repaid me evils, let me deservedly fall empty before my enemies. Let the enemy pursue my soul, and take it, and tread down my life on the earth, and bring down my glory to the dust. Rise up, O LORD, in thy anger: and be thou exalted in the borders of my enemies. And arise, O LORD my God, in the precept which thou hast commanded: And a congregation of people shall surround thee. And for their sakes return thou on high. The Lord judgeth the people. Judge me, O LORD, according to my justice, and according to my innocence in me. The wickedness of sinners shall be brought to nought: and thou shalt direct the just: the searcher of hearts and reins is God. Just is my help from the LORD: who saveth the upright of heart. God is a just judge, strong and patient: is he angry every day? Except you will be converted, he will brandish his sword: he hath bent his bow and made it ready. And in it he hath prepared the instruments of death, he hath made ready his arrows for them that burn. Behold he hath been in labour with injustice; he hath conceived sorrow, and brought forth iniquity. He hath opened a pit and dug it; and he is fallen into the hole he made. His sorrow shall be turned on his own head: and his iniquity shall come down upon his crown. I will give glory to the LORD according to his justice: and will sing to the name of the LORD the Most High.

8

Domine, dominus noster

O LORD our LORD, how admirable is thy name in the whole earth! For thy magnificence is elevated above the heavens. Out of the mouth of infants and of sucklings thou hast perfected praise, because of thy enemies, that thou mayst destroy the enemy and the avenger. For I will behold thy heavens, the works of thy fingers: the moon and the stars which thou hast founded. What is man that thou art mindful of him? or the son of man that thou visitest him? Thou hast made him a little less than the angels, thou hast crowned him with glory and honour: And hast set him over the works of thy hands. Thou hast subjected all things under his feet, all sheep and oxen: moreover the beasts also of the fields. The birds of the air, and the fishes of the sea, that pass through the paths of the sea. O LORD our LORD, how admirable is thy name in all the earth!

9

Confitebor tibi, Domine

I will give praise to thee, O LORD, with my whole heart: I will relate all thy wonders. I will be glad and rejoice in thee: I will sing to thy name, O thou Most High. When my enemy shall be turned back: they shall be weakened and perish before thy face. For thou hast maintained my judgment and my cause: thou hast sat on the throne, who judgest justice. Thou hast rebuked the Gentiles, and the wicked one hath perished: thou hast blotted out their name for ever and ever. The swords of the enemy have failed unto the end: and their cities thou hast destroyed. Their memory hath perished with a noise. But the LORD remaineth forever. He hath prepared his throne in judgment: And he shall judge the world in equity, he shall judge the people in justice. And the LORD is become a refuge for the poor: a helper in due time in tribulation. And let them trust in thee who know thy name: for thou hast not forsaken them that seek thee, O LORD. Sing ye to the LORD, who dwelleth in Zion: declare his ways among the Gentiles: For requiring their blood he hath remembered them: he hath not forgotten the cry of the poor. Have mercy on me, O LORD: see my humiliation which I suffer from my enemies. Thou that liftest me up from the gates of death, that I may declare all thy praises in the gates of the daughter of Zion. I will rejoice in thy salvation: the Gentiles have stuck fast in the destruction which they have prepared. Their foot hath been taken in the very snare which they hid. The Lord shall be known when he executeth judgments: the sinner hath been caught in the works of his own hands. The wicked shall be turned into hell, all the nations that forget God. For the poor man shall not be forgotten to the end: the patience of the poor shall not perish forever. Arise, O LORD, let not man be strengthened: let the Gentiles be judged in thy sight. Appoint, O LORD, a lawgiver over them: that the Gentiles may know themselves to be but men.

10

In Domino confido

In the LORD I put my trust: how then do you say to my soul: Get thee away from hence to the mountain like a sparrow? For, lo, the wicked have bent their bow; they have prepared their arrows in the quiver; to shoot in the dark the upright of heart. For they have destroyed the things which thou hast made: but what has the just man done? The LORD is in his holy temple, the LORD's throne is in heaven. His eyes look on the poor man: his eyelids examine the sons of men. The LORD trieth the just and the wicked: but he that loveth iniquity hateth his own soul. He shall rain snares upon sinners: fire and brimstone and storms of winds shall be the portion of their cup. For the LORD is just, and hath loved justice: his countenance hath beheld righteousness.

11

Salvum me fac

Save me, O LORD, for there is now no saint: truths are decayed from among the children of men. They have spoken vain things everyone to his neighbour: with deceitful lips, and with a double heart have they spoken. May the LORD destroy all deceitful lips, and the tongue that speaketh proud things. Who have said: We will magnify our tongue; our lips are our own; who is LORD over us? By reason of the misery of the needy, and the groans of the poor, now will I arise, saith the LORD. I win set him in safety; I will deal confidently in his regard. The words of the LORD are pure words: as silver tried by the fire, purged from the earth refined seven times. Thou, O LORD, wilt preserve us: and keep us from this generation forever. The wicked walk round about: according to thy highness, thou hast multiplied the children of men.

12

Usquequo, Domine.

How long, O LORD, wilt thou forget me unto the end? how long dost thou turn away thy face from me? How long shall I take counsels in my soul, sorrow in my heart all the day? How long shall my enemy be exalted over me? Consider, and hear me, O LORD my God. Enlighten my eyes that I never sleep in death: Lest at any time my enemy say: I have prevailed against him. They that trouble me will rejoice when I am moved: But I have trusted in thy mercy. My heart shall rejoice in thy salvation: I will sing to the LORD, who giveth me good things: yea I will sing to the name of the LORD the Most High.

Second Session

13

Dixit insipiens

The fool hath said in his heart: There is no God, They are corrupt, and are become abominable in their ways: there is none that doth good, no not one. The LORD hath looked down from heaven upon the children of men, to see if there be any that understand and seek God. They are all gone aside, they are become unprofitable together: there is none that doth good, no not one. Their throat is an open sepulchre: with their tongues they acted deceitfully; the poison of asps is under their lips. Their mouth is full of cursing and bitterness; their feet are swift to shed blood. Destruction and unhappiness in their ways: and the way of peace they have not known: there is no fear of God before their eyes. Shall not all they know that work iniquity, who devour my people as they eat bread? They have not called upon the LORD: there have they trembled for fear, where there was no fear. For the LORD is in the just generation: you have confounded the counsel of the poor man, but the LORD is his hope. Who shall give out of Zion the salvation of Israel? when the LORD shall have turned away the captivity of his people, Jacob shall rejoice and Israel shall be glad.

14

Domine, quis habitabit

LORD, who shall dwell in thy tabernacle? or who shall rest in thy holy hill? He that walketh without blemish, and worketh justice: He that speaketh truth in his heart, who hath not used deceit in his tongue: Nor hath done evil to his neighbour: nor taken up a reproach against his neighbours. In his sight the malignant is brought to nothing: but he glorifieth them that fear the LORD. He that sweareth to his neighbour, and deceiveth not; He that hath not put out his money to usury, nor taken bribes against the innocent: He that doth these things shall not be moved forever.

15

Conserva me, Domine

Preserve me, O LORD, for I have put trust in thee. I have said to the LORD, thou art my God, for thou hast no need of my goods. To the saints, who are in his land, he hath made wonderful all my desires in them. Their infirmities were multiplied: afterwards they made haste. I will not gather together their meetings for blood offerings: nor will I be mindful of their names by my lips. The LORD is the portion of my inheritance and of my cup: it is thou that wilt restore my inheritance to me. The lines are fallen unto me in goodly places: for my inheritance is goodly to me. I will bless the LORD, who hath given me understanding: moreover my reins also have corrected me even till night. I set the LORD always in my sight: for he is at my right hand, that I be not moved. Therefore my heart hath been glad, and my tongue hath rejoiced: moreover my flesh also shall rest in hope. Because thou wilt not leave my soul in hell; nor wilt thou give thy holy one to see corruption. Thou hast made known to me the ways of life, thou shalt fill me with joy with thy countenance: at thy right hand are delights even to the end.

16

Exaudi, Domine, justitiam

Hear, O LORD, my justice: attend to my supplication. Give ear unto my prayer, which proceedeth not from deceitful lips. Let my judgment come forth from thy countenance: let thy eyes behold the things that are equitable. Thou hast proved my heart, and visited it by night, thou hast tried me by fire: and iniquity hath not been found in me. That my mouth may not speak the works of men: for the sake of the words of thy lips, I have kept hard ways. Perfect thou my goings in thy paths: that my footsteps be not moved. I have cried to thee, for thou, O God, hast heard me: O incline thy ear unto me, and hear my words. Shew forth thy wonderful mercies; thou who savest them that trust in thee. From them that resist thy right hand keep me, as the apple of thy eye. Protect me under the shadow of thy wings. From the face of the wicked who have afflicted me. My enemies have surrounded my soul: They have shut up their fat: their mouth hath spoken proudly. They have cast me forth and now they have surrounded me: they have set their eyes bowing down to the earth. They have taken me, as a lion prepared for the prey; and as a young lion dwelling in secret places. Arise, O LORD, disappoint him and supplant him; deliver my soul from the wicked one: thy sword from the enemies of thy hand. O LORD, divide them from the few of the earth in their life: their belly is filled from thy hidden stores. They are full of children: and they have left to their little ones the rest of their substance. But as for me, I will appear before thy sight in justice: I shall be satisfied when thy glory shall appear.

17

Diligam te, Domine

I will love thee, O LORD, my strength: The LORD is my firmament, my refuge, and my deliverer. My God is my helper, and in him will I put my trust. My protector and the horn of my salvation, and my support. Praising I will call upon the LORD: and I shall be saved from my enemies. The sorrows of death surrounded me: and the torrents of iniquity troubled me. The sorrows of hell encompassed me: and the snares of death prevented me. In my affliction I called upon the LORD, and I cried to my God: And he heard my voice from his holy temple: and my cry before him came into his ears. The earth shook and trembled: the foundations of the mountains were troubled and were moved, because he was angry with them. There went up a smoke in his wrath: and a fire flamed from his face: coals were kindled by it. He bowed the heavens, and came down: and darkness was under his feet. And he ascended upon the cherubim, and he flew; he flew upon the wings of the winds. And he made darkness his covert, his pavilion round about him: dark waters in the clouds of the air. At the brightness that was before him the clouds passed, hail and coals of fire. And the LORD thundered from heaven, and the highest gave his voice: hail and coals of fire. And he sent forth his arrows, and he scattered them: he multiplied lightnings, and troubled them. Then the fountains of waters appeared, and the foundations of the world were discovered: At thy rebuke, O LORD, at the blast of the spirit of thy wrath. He sent from on high, and took me: and received me out of many waters. He delivered me from my strongest enemies, and from them that hated me: for they were too strong for me. They prevented me in the day of my affliction: and the LORD became my protector. And he brought me forth into a large place: he saved me, because he was well pleased with me. And the LORD will reward me according to my justice; and will repay me according to the cleanness of my hands: Because I have kept the ways of the LORD; and have not done wickedly against my God. For till his judgments are in my sight: and his justices I have not put away from me. And I shall be spotless with him: and shall keep myself from my iniquity. And the LORD will reward me according to my justice; and according to the cleanness of my hands before his eyes. With the holy, thou wilt be holy; and with the innocent man thou wilt be innocent. And with the elect thou wilt be elect: and with the perverse thou wilt be perverted. For thou wilt save the humble people; but wilt bring down the eyes of the proud. For thou lightest my lamp, O LORD: O my God enlighten my darkness. For by thee I shall be delivered from temptation; and through my God I shall go over a wall. As for my God, his way is undefiled: the words of the LORD are fire tried: he is the protector of all that trust in him. For who is God but the LORD? or who is God but our God? God who hath girt me with strength; and made my way blameless. Who hath made my feet like the feet of harts: and who setteth me upon high places. Who teacheth my hands to war: and thou hast made my arms like a brazen bow. And thou hast given me the protection of thy salvation: and thy right hand hath held me up: And thy discipline hath corrected me unto the end: and thy discipline, the same shall teach me. Thou hast enlarged my steps under me; and my feet are not weakened. I will pursue after my enemies, and overtake them: and I will not turn again till they are consumed. I will break them, and they shall not be able to stand: they shall fall under my feet. And thou hast girded me with strength unto battle; and hast subdued under me them that rose up against me. And thou hast made my enemies turn their back upon me, and hast destroyed them that hated me. They cried, but there was none to save them, to the LORD: but he heard them not. And I shall beat them as small as the dust before the wind; I shall bring them to nought, like the dirt in the streets. Thou wilt deliver me from the contradictions of the people: thou wilt make me head of the Gentiles. A people, which I knew not, hath served me: at the hearing of the ear they have obeyed me. The children that are strangers have lied to me, strange children have faded away, and have halted from their paths. The LORD liveth, and blessed be my God, and let the God of my salvation be exalted: O God, who avengest me, and subduest the people under me, my deliverer from my enemies. And thou wilt lift me up above them that rise up against me: from the unjust man thou wilt deliver me. Therefore will I give glory to thee, O LORD, among the nations, and I will sing a psalm to thy name. Giving great deliverance to his king, and shewing mercy to David his anointed: and to his seed forever.

18

Coeli enarrant

The heavens shew forth the glory of God, and the firmament declareth the work of his hands. Day to day uttereth speech, and night to night sheweth knowledge. There are no speeches nor languages, where their voices are not heard. Their sound hath gone forth into all the earth: and their words unto the ends of the world. He hath set his tabernacle in the sun: and he, as a bridegroom coming out of his bride chamber, Hath rejoiced as a giant to run the way: His going out is from the end of heaven, And his circuit even to the end thereof: and there is no one that can hide himself from his heat. The law of the LORD is unspotted, converting souls: the testimony of the LORD is faithful, giving wisdom to little ones. The justices of the Lord are right, rejoicing hearts: the commandment of the LORD is lightsome, enlightening the eyes. The fear of the LORD is holy, enduring forever and ever: the judgments of the LORD are true, justified in themselves. More to be desired than gold and many precious stones: and sweeter than honey and the honeycomb. For thy servant keepeth them, and in keeping them there is a great reward. Who can understand sins? from my secret ones cleanse me, O LORD: And from those of others spare thy servant. If they shall have no dominion over me, then shall I be without spot: and I shall be cleansed from the greatest sin. And the words of my mouth shall be such as may please: and the meditation of my heart always in thy sight. O LORD, my helper, and my redeemer.

19

Exaudiat te Dominus

May the LORD hear thee in the day of tribulation: may the name of the God of Jacob protect thee. May he send thee help from the sanctuary: and defend thee out of Zion. May he be mindful of all thy sacrifices: and may thy whole burnt offering be made fat. May he give thee according to thy own heart; and confirm all thy counsels. We will rejoice in thy salvation;

and in the name of our God we shall be exalted. The LORD fulfill all thy petitions: now have I known that the LORD hath saved his anointed. He will hear him from his holy heaven: the salvation of his right hand is in powers. Some trust in chariots, and some in horses: but we will call upon the name of the LORD our God. They are bound, and have fallen; but we are risen, and are set upright. O LORD, save the king: and hear us in the day that we shall call upon thee.

20

Domine, in virtute

In thy strength, O LORD, the king shall joy; and in thy salvation he shall rejoice exceedingly. Thou hast given him his heart's desire: and hast not withholden from him the will of his lips. For thou hast prevented him with blessings of sweetness: thou hast set on his head a crown of precious stones. He asked life of thee: and thou hast given him length of days forever and ever. His glory is great in thy salvation: glory and great beauty shalt thou lay upon him. For thou shalt give him to be a blessing for ever and ever: thou shalt make him joyful in gladness with thy countenance. For the king hopeth in the LORD: and through the mercy of the Most High he shall not be moved. Let thy hand be found by all thy enemies: let thy right hand find out all them that hate thee. Thou shalt make them as an oven of fire, in the time of thy anger: the LORD shall trouble them in his wrath, and fire shall devour them. Their fruit shalt thou destroy from the earth: and their seed from among the children of men. For they have intended evils against thee: they have devised counsels which they have not been able to establish. For thou shalt make them turn their back: in thy remnants thou shalt prepare their face. Be thou exalted, O LORD, in thy own strength: we will sing and praise thy power.

21

Deus Deus meus

O God my God, look upon me: why hast thou forsaken me? Far from my salvation are the words of my sins. O my God, I shall cry by day, and thou wilt not hear: and by night, and it shall not be reputed as folly in me. But thou dwellest in the holy place, the praise of Israel. In thee have our fathers hoped: they have hoped, and thou hast delivered them. They cried to thee, and they were saved: they trusted in thee, and were not confounded. But I am a worm, and no man: the reproach of men, and the outcast of the people. All they that saw me have laughed me to scorn: they have spoken with the lips and wagged the head. He hoped in the LORD, let him deliver him: let him save him, seeing he delighteth in him. For thou art he that hast drawn me out of the womb: my hope from the breasts of my mother. I was cast upon thee from the womb. From my mother's womb thou art my God, depart not from me. For tribulation is very near: for there is none to help me. Many calves have surrounded me: fat bulls have besieged me. They have opened their mouths against me, as a lion ravening and roaring. I am poured out like water; and all my bones are scattered. My heart is become like wax melting in the midst of my bowels. My strength is dried up like a potsherd, and my tongue hath cleaved to my jaws: and thou hast brought me down into the dust of death. For many dogs have encompassed me: the council of the malignant hath besieged me. They have dug my hands and feet. They have numbered all my bones. And they have looked and stared upon me. They parted my garments amongst them; and upon my vesture they cast lots. But thou, O LORD, remove not thy help to a distance from me; look towards my defence. Deliver, O God, my soul from the sword: my only one from the hand of the dog. Save me from the lion's mouth; and my lowness from the horns of the unicorns. I will declare thy name to my brethren: in the midst of the church will I praise thee. Ye that fear the LORD, praise him: all ye the seed of Jacob, glorify him. Let all the seed of Israel fear him: because he hath not slighted nor despised the supplication of the poor man. Neither hath he turned away his face from me: and when I cried to him he heard me. With thee is my praise in a great church: I will pay my vows in the sight of them that fear him. The poor shall eat and shall be filled: and they shall praise the LORD that seek him: their hearts shall live forever and ever. All the ends of the earth shall remember, and shall be converted to the LORD: And all the kindreds of the Gentiles shall adore in his sight. For the kingdom is the LORD's; and he shall have dominion over the nations. All the fat ones of the earth have eaten and have adored: all they that go down to the earth shall fall before him. And to him my soul shall live: and my seed shall serve him. There shall be declared to the LORD a generation to come: and the heavens shall shew forth his justice to a people that shall be born, which the LORD hath made.

22

Dominus regit me

The LORD ruleth me: and I shall want nothing. He hath set me in a place of pasture. He hath brought me up, on the water of refreshment: He hath converted my soul. He hath led me on the paths of justice, for his own name's sake. For though I should walk in the midst of the shadow of death, I will fear no evils, for thou art with me. Thy rod and thy staff, they have comforted me. Thou hast prepared a table before me against them that afflict me. Thou hast anointed my head with oil; and my chalice which inebriateth me, how goodly is it! And thy mercy will follow me all the days of my life. And that I may dwell in the house of the Lord unto length of days.

23

Domini est terra

The earth is the LORD's and the fulness thereof: the world, and all they that dwell therein. For he hath founded it upon the seas; and hath prepared it upon the rivers. Who shall ascend into the mountain of the LORD: or who shall stand in his holy place? The innocent in hands, and clean of heart, who hath not taken his soul in vain, nor sworn deceitfully to his neighbour. He shall receive a blessing from the LORD, and mercy from God his Saviour. This is the generation of them that seek him, of them that seek the face of the God of Jacob. Lift up your gates, O ye princes, and be ye lifted up, O eternal gates: and the King of Glory shall enter in. Who is this King of Glory? the LORD who is strong and mighty: the LORD mighty in battle. Lift up your gates, O ye princes, and be ye lifted up, O eternal gates: and the King of Glory shall enter in. Who is this King of Glory? the Lord of hosts, he is the King of Glory.

24

Ad te, Domine, levavi

To thee, O LORD, have I lifted up my soul. In thee, O my God, I put my trust; let me not be ashamed. Neither let my enemies laugh at me: for none of them that wait on thee shall be confounded. Let all them be confounded that act unjust things without cause. shew, O LORD, thy ways to me, and teach me thy paths. Direct me in thy truth, and teach me; for thou art God my Saviour; and on thee have I waited all the day long. Remember, O LORD, thy bowels of compassion; and thy mercies that are from the beginning of the world. The sins of my youth and my ignorances do not remember. According to thy mercy remember thou me: for thy goodness' sake, O LORD. The LORD is sweet and righteous: therefore he will give a law to sinners in the way. He will guide the mild in judgment: he will teach the meek his ways. All the ways of the LORD are mercy and truth, to them that seek after his covenant and his testimonies. For thy name's sake, O LORD, thou wilt pardon my sin: for it is great. Who is the man that feareth the LORD? He hath appointed him a law in the way he hath chosen. His soul shall dwell in good things: and his seed shall inherit the land. The LORD is a firmament to them that fear him: and his covenant shall be made manifest to them. My eyes are ever towards the LORD: for he shall pluck my feet out of the snare. Look thou upon me, and have mercy on me; for I am alone and poor. The troubles of my heart are multiplied: deliver me from my necessities. See my abjection and my labour; and forgive me all my sins. Consider my enemies for they are multiplied, and have hated me with an unjust hatred. Keep thou my soul, and deliver me: I shall not be ashamed, for I have hoped in thee. The innocent and the upright have adhered to me: because I have waited on thee. Deliver Israel, O God, from all his tribulations.

Session Three

25

Judica me, Domine

Judge me, O LORD, for I have walked in my innocence: and I have put my trust in the LORD, and shall not be weakened. Prove me, O LORD, and try me; burn my reins and my heart. For thy mercy is before my eyes; and I am well pleased with thy truth. I have not sat with the council of vanity: neither will I go in with the doers of unjust things. I have hated the assembly of the malignant; and with the wicked I will not sit. I will wash my hands among the innocent; and will compass thy altar, O LORD: That I may hear the voice of thy praise: and tell of all thy wondrous works. I have loved, O LORD, the beauty of thy house; and the place where thy glory dwelleth. Take not away my soul, O God, with the wicked: nor my life with bloody men: In whose hands are iniquities: their right hand is filled with gifts. But as for me, I have walked in my innocence: redeem me, and have mercy on me. My foot hath stood in the direct way: in the churches I will bless thee, O LORD.

26

Dominus illuminatio

The LORD is my light and my salvation, whom shall I fear? The LORD is the protector of my life: of whom shall I be afraid? Whilst the wicked draw near against me, to eat my flesh. My enemies that trouble me, have themselves been weakened, and have fallen. If armies in camp should stand together against me, my heart shall not fear. If a battle should rise up against me, in this will I be confident. One thing I have asked of the LORD, this will I seek after; that I may dwell in the house of the LORD all the days of my life. That I may see the delight of the LORD, and may visit his temple. For he hath hidden me in his tabernacle; in the day of evils, he hath protected me in the secret place of his tabernacle. He hath exalted me upon a rock: and now he hath lifted up my head above my enemies. I have gone round, and have offered up in his tabernacle a sacrifice of jubilation: I will sing, and recite a psalm to the LORD. Hear, O LORD, my voice, with which I have cried to thee: have mercy on me and hear me. My heart hath said to thee: My face hath sought thee: thy face, O LORD, will I still seek. Turn not away thy face from me; decline not in thy wrath from thy servant. Be thou my helper, forsake me not; do not thou despise me, O God my Saviour. For my father and my mother have left me: but the Lord hath taken me up. Set me, O LORD, a law in thy way, and guide me in the right path, because of my enemies. Deliver me not over to the will of them that trouble me; for unjust witnesses have risen up against me; and iniquity hath lied to itself. I believe to see the good things of the LORD in the land of the living. Expect the LORD, do manfully, and let thy heart take courage, and wait thou for the LORD.

27

Ad te, Domine, clamabo

Unto thee will I cry, O LORD: O my God, be not thou silent to me: lest thou be silent to me, I become like them that go down into the pit. Hear, O LORD, the voice of my supplication, when I pray to thee; when I lift up my hands to thy holy temple. Draw me not away together with the wicked; and with the workers of iniquity destroy me not: Who speak peace with their neighbour, but evils are in their hearts. Give them according to their works, and according to the wickedness of their inventions. According to the works of their hands give thou to them: render to them their reward. Because they have not understood the works of the LORD, and the operations of his hands: thou shalt destroy them, and shalt not build them up. Blessed be the LORD, for he hath heard the voice of my supplication. The LORD is my helper and my protector: in him hath my heart confided, and I have been helped. And my flesh hath flourished again, and with my will I will give praise to him. The LORD is the strength of his people, and the protector of the salvation of his anointed. Save, O LORD, thy people, and bless thy inheritance: and rule them and exalt them forever.

28

Afferte Domino

Bring to the LORD, O ye children of God: bring to the LORD the offspring of rams. Bring to the LORD glory and honour: bring to the LORD glory to his name: adore ye the LORD in his holy court. The voice of the LORD is upon the waters; the God of majesty hath thundered, The LORD is upon many waters. The voice of the LORD is in power; the voice of the Lord in magnificence. The voice of the LORD breaketh the cedars: yea, the LORD shall break the cedars of Libanus. And shall reduce them to pieces, as a calf of Libanus, and as the beloved son of unicorns. The voice of the LORD divideth the flame of fire: The voice of the LORD shaketh the desert: and the LORD shall shake the desert of Cades. The voice of the LORD prepareth the stags: and he will discover the thick woods: and in his temple all shall speak his glory. The LORD maketh the flood to dwell: and the LORD shall sit king forever. The LORD will give strength to his people: the Lord will bless his people with peace.

29

Exaltabo te, Domine

I will extol thee, O LORD, for thou hast upheld me: and hast not made my enemies to rejoice over me. O LORD my God, I have cried to thee, and thou hast healed me. Thou hast brought forth, O LORD, my soul from hell: thou hast saved me from them that go down into the pit. Sing to the LORD, O ye his saints: and give praise to the memory of his holiness. For wrath is in his indignation; and life in his good will. In the evening weeping shall have place, and in the morning gladness. And in my abundance I said: I shall never be moved. O LORD, in thy favour, thou gavest strength to my beauty. Thou turnedst away thy face from me, and I became troubled. To thee, O LORD, will I cry: and I will make supplication to my God. What profit is there in my blood, whilst I go down to corruption? Shall dust confess to thee, or declare thy truth? The LORD hath heard, and hath had mercy on me: the LORD became my helper. Thou hast turned for me my mourning into joy: thou hast cut my sackcloth, and hast compassed me with gladness: To the end that my glory may sing to thee, and I may not regret: O LORD my God, I will give praise to thee forever.

30

In te, Domine, speravi

In thee, O LORD, have I hoped, let me never be confounded: deliver me in thy justice. Bow down thy ear to me: make haste to deliver me. Be thou unto me a God, a protector, and a house of refuge, to save me. For thou art my strength and my refuge; and for thy name's sake thou wilt lead me, and nourish me. Thou wilt bring me out of this snare, which they have hidden for me: for thou art my protector. Into thy hands I commend my spirit: thou hast redeemed me, O LORD, the God of truth. Thou hast hated them that regard vanities, to no purpose. But I have hoped in the LORD: I will be glad and rejoice in thy mercy. For thou hast regarded my humility, thou hast saved my soul out of distresses. And thou hast not shut me up in the hands of the enemy: thou hast set my feet in a spacious place. And thou hast not shut me up in the hands of the enemy: thou hast set my feet in a spacious place. Have mercy on me, O LORD, for I am afflicted: my eye is troubled with wrath, my soul, and my belly: For my life is wasted with grief: and my years in sighs. My strength is weakened through poverty and my bones are disturbed. I am become a reproach among all my enemies, and very much to my neighbours; and a fear to my acquaintance. They that saw me without fled from me. I am forgotten as one dead from the heart. I am become as a vessel that is destroyed. For I have heard the blame of many that dwell round about. While they assembled together against me, they consulted to take away my life. But I have put my trust in thee, O LORD: I said: Thou art my God. My lots are in thy hands. Deliver me out of the hands of my enemies; and from them that persecute me. Make thy face to shine upon thy servant; save me in thy mercy. Let me not be confounded, O LORD, for I have called upon thee. Let the wicked be ashamed, and be brought down to hell. Let deceitful lips be made dumb. Which speak iniquity against the just, with pride and abuse. O how great is the multitude of thy sweetness, O LORD, which thou hast hidden for them that fear thee! Which thou hast wrought for them that hope in thee, in the sight of the sons of men. Thou shalt hide them in the secret of thy face, from the disturbance of men. Thou shalt protect them in thy tabernacle from the contradiction of tongues. Blessed be the LORD, for he hath shewn his wonderful mercy to me in a fortified city. But I said in the excess of my mind: I am cast away from before thy eyes. Therefore thou hast heard the voice of my prayer, when I cried to thee. O love the LORD, all ye his saints: for the LORD will require truth, and will repay them abundantly that act proudly. Do ye manfully, and let your heart be strengthened, all ye that hope in the LORD.

31

Beati quorum

Blessed are they whose iniquities are forgiven, and whose sins are covered. Blessed is the man to whom the LORD hath not imputed sin, and in whose spirit there is no guile. Because I was silent my bones grew old; whilst I cried out all the day long. For day and night thy hand was heavy upon me: I am turned in my anguish, whilst the thorn is fastened. I have acknowledged my sin to thee, and my injustice I have not concealed. I said I will confess against myself my injustice to the LORD: and thou hast forgiven the wickedness of my sin. For this shall every one that is holy pray to thee in a seasonable time. And yet in a flood of many waters, they shall not come nigh unto him. Thou art my refuge from the trouble which hath encompassed me: my joy, deliver me from them that surround me. I will give thee understanding, and I will instruct thee in this way, in which thou shalt go: I will fix my eyes upon thee. Do not become like the horse and the mule, who have no understanding. With bit and bridle bind fast their jaws, who come not near unto thee. Many are the scourges of the sinner, but mercy shall encompass him that hopeth in the LORD. Be glad in the LORD, and rejoice, ye just, and glory, all ye right of heart.

32

Exultate, justi

Rejoice in the LORD, O ye just: praise becometh the upright. Give praise to the LORD on the harp; sing to him with the psaltery, the instrument of ten strings. Sing to him a new canticle, sing well unto him with a loud noise. For the word of the LORD is right, and all his works are done with faithfulness. He loveth mercy and judgment; the earth is full of the mercy of the LORD. By the word of the LORD the heavens were established; and all the power of them by the spirit of his mouth: Gathering together the waters of the sea, as in a vessel; laying up the depths in storehouses. Let all the earth fear the LORD, and let all the inhabitants of the world be in awe of him. For he spoke and they were made: he commanded and they were created. The LORD bringeth to naught the counsels of nations; and he rejecteth the devices of people, and casteth away the counsels of princes. But the counsel of the LORD standeth forever: the thoughts of his heart to all generations. Blessed is the nation whose God is the LORD: the people whom he hath chosen for his inheritance. The LORD hath looked from heaven: he hath beheld all the sons of men. From his habitation which he hath prepared, he hath looked upon all that dwell on the earth. He who hath made the hearts of every one of them: who understandeth all their works. The king is not saved by a great army: nor shall the giant be saved by his own great strength. Vain is the horse for safety: neither shall he be saved by the abundance of his strength. Behold the eyes of the LORD are on them that fear him: and on them that hope in his mercy. To deliver their souls from death; and feed them in famine. Our soul waiteth for the LORD: for he is our helper and protector. For in him our heart shall rejoice: and in his holy name we have trusted. Let thy mercy, O LORD, be upon us, as we have hoped in thee.

33

Benedicam Dominum

I will bless the LORD at all times, his praise shall be always in my mouth. In the LORD shall my soul be praised: let the meek hear and rejoice. O magnify the LORD with me; and let us extol his name together. I sought the LORD, and he heard me; and he delivered me from all my troubles. Come ye to him and be enlightened: and your faces shall not be confounded. This poor man cried, and the LORD heard him: and saved him out of all his troubles. The angel of the LORD shall encamp round about them that fear him: and shall deliver them. O taste, and see that the LORD is sweet: blessed is the man that hopeth in him. Fear the LORD, all ye his saints: for there is no want to them that fear him. The rich have wanted, and have suffered hunger: but they that seek the LORD shall not be deprived of any good. Come, children, hearken to me: I will teach you the fear of the LORD. Who is the man that desireth life: who loveth to see good days? Keep thy tongue from evil, and thy lips from speaking guile. Turn away from evil and do good: seek after peace and pursue it. The eyes of the LORD are upon the just: and his ears unto their prayers. But the countenance of the LORD is against them that do evil things: to cut off the remembrance of them from the earth. The just cried, and the LORD heard them: and delivered them out of all their troubles. The LORD is nigh unto them that are of a contrite heart: and he will save the humble of spirit. Many are the afflictions of the just; but out of them all will the LORD deliver them. The LORD keepeth all their bones, not one of them shall be broken. The death of the wicked is very evil: and they that hate the just shall be guilty. The LORD will redeem the souls of his servants: and none of them that trust in him shall offend.

34

Judica, Domine, nocentes me

Judge thou, O LORD, them that wrong me: overthrow them that fight against me. Take hold of arms and shield: and rise up to help me. Bring out the sword, and shut up the way against them that persecute me: say to my soul: I am thy salvation. Let them be confounded and ashamed that seek after my soul. Let them be turned back and be confounded that devise against me. Let them become as dust before the wind: and let the angel of the LORD straiten them. Let their way become dark and slippery; and let the angel of the LORD pursue them. For without cause they have hidden their net for me unto destruction: without cause they have upbraided my soul. Let the snare which he knoweth not come upon him: and let the net which he hath hidden catch him: and into that very snare let them fall. But my soul shall rejoice in the LORD; and shall be delighted in his salvation. All my bones shall say: LORD, who is like to thee? Who deliverest the poor from the hand of them that are stronger than he; the needy and the poor from them that strip him. Unjust witnesses rising up have asked me things I knew not. They repaid me evil for good: to the depriving me of my soul. But as for me, when they were troublesome to me, I was clothed with haircloth. I humbled my soul with fasting; and my prayer shall be turned into my bosom. As a neighbour and as an own brother, so did I please: as one mourning and sorrowful so was I humbled. But they rejoiced against me, and came together: scourges were gathered together upon me, and I knew not. They were separated, and repented not: they tempted me, they scoffed at me with scorn: they gnashed upon me with their teeth. LORD, when wilt thou look upon me? rescue thou my soul from their malice: my only one from the lions. I will give thanks to thee in a great church; I will praise thee in a strong people. Let not them that are my enemies wrongfully rejoice over me: who have hated me without cause, and wink with the eyes. For they spoke indeed peaceably to me; and speaking in the anger of the earth they devised guile. And they opened their mouth wide against me; they said: Well done, well done, our eyes have seen it. Thou hast seen, O LORD, be not thou silent: O LORD, depart not from me. Arise, and be attentive to my judgment: to my cause, my God, and my LORD. Judge me, O LORD my God according to thy justice, and let them not rejoice over me. Let them not say in their hearts: It is well, it is well, to our mind: neither let them say: We have swallowed him up. Let them blush: and be ashamed together, who rejoice at my evils. Let them be clothed with confusion and shame, who speak great things against me. Let them rejoice and be glad, who are well pleased with my justice, and let them say always: The LORD be magnified, who delights in the peace of his servant. And my tongue shall meditate thy justice, thy praise all the day long.

35

Dixit injustus

The unjust hath said within himself, that he would sin: there is no fear of God before his eyes. For in his sight he hath done deceitfully, that his iniquity may be found unto hatred. The words of his mouth are iniquity and guile: he would not understand that he might do well. He hath devised iniquity on his bed, he hath set himself on every way that is not good: but evil he hath not hated. O LORD, thy mercy is in heaven, and thy truth reacheth, even to the clouds. Thy justice is as the mountains of God, thy judgments are a great deep. Men and beasts thou wilt preserve, O LORD: O how hast thou multiplied thy mercy, O God! But the children of men shall put their trust under the covert of thy wings. They shall be inebriated with the plenty of thy house; and thou shalt make them drink of the torrent of thy pleasure. For with thee is the fountain of life; and in thy light we shall see light. Extend thy mercy to them that know thee, and thy justice to them that are right in heart. Let not the foot of pride come to me, and let not the hand of the sinner move me. There the workers of iniquity are fallen, they are cast out, and could not stand.

36

Noli aemulari

Be not emulous of evildoers; nor envy them that work iniquity. For they shall shortly wither away as grass, and as the green herbs shall quickly fall. Trust in the LORD, and do good, and dwell in the land, and thou shalt be fed with its riches. Delight in the LORD, and he will give thee the requests of thy heart. Commit thy way to the LORD, and trust in him, and he will do it. And he will bring forth thy justice as the light, and thy judgment as the noonday. Be subject to the LORD and pray to him Envy not the man who prospereth in his way; the man who doth unjust things. Cease from anger, and leave rage; have no emulation to do evil. For the evildoers shall be cut off: but they that wait upon the LORD shall inherit the land. For yet a little while, and the wicked shall not be: and thou shalt seek his place, and shalt not find it. But the meek shall inherit the land, and shall delight in abundance of peace. The sinner shall watch the just man: and shall gnash upon him with his teeth. But the LORD shall laugh at him: for he foreseeth that his day shall come. The wicked have drawn out the sword: they have bent their bow. To cast down the poor and needy, to kill the upright of heart. Let their sword enter into their own hearts, and let their bow be broken. Better is a little to the just, than the great riches of the wicked. For the arms of the wicked shall be broken in pieces; but the LORD strengtheneth the just. The LORD knoweth the days of undefiled; and their inheritance shall be forever. They shall not be confounded in the evil time; and in the days of famine they shall be filled: Because the wicked shall perish. And the enemies of the LORD, presently after they shall be honoured and exalted, shall come to nothing and vanish like smoke. The sinner shall borrow, and not pay again; but the just sheweth mercy and shall give. For such as bless him shall inherit the land: but such as curse him shall perish. With the LORD shall the steps of a man be directed, and he shall like well his way. When he shall fall he shall not be bruised, for the LORD putteth his hand under him. I have been young, and now am old; and I have not seen the just forsaken, nor his seed seeking bread. He sheweth mercy, and lendeth all the day long; and his seed shall be in blessing. Decline from evil and do good, and dwell forever and ever. For the LORD loveth judgment, and will not forsake his saints: they shall be preserved forever. The unjust shall be punished, and the seed of the wicked shall perish. But the just shall inherit the land, and shall dwell therein forevermore. The mouth of the just shall meditate wisdom: and his tongue shall speak judgment. The law of his God is in his heart, and his steps shall not be supplanted. The wicked watcheth the just man, and seeketh to put him to death, But the LORD will not leave him in his hands; nor condemn him when he shall be judged. Expect the LORD and keep his way: and he will exalt thee to inherit the land: when the sinners shall perish thou shalt see. I have seen the wicked highly exalted, and lifted up like the cedars of Libanus. And I passed by, and lo, he was not: and I sought him and his place was not found. Keep innocence, and behold justice: for there are remnants for the peaceable man. But the unjust shall be destroyed together: the remnants of the wicked shall perish. But the salvation of the just is from the LORD, and he is their protector in the time of trouble. And the LORD will help them and deliver them: and he will rescue them from the wicked, and save them, because they have hoped in him.

Session Four

37

Domine, ne in furore

Rebuke me not, O LORD, in thy indignation; nor chastise me in thy wrath. For thy arrows are fastened in me: and thy hand hath been strong upon me. There is no health in my flesh, because of thy wrath: there is no peace for my bones, because of my sins. For my iniquities are gone over my head: and as a heavy burden are become heavy upon me. My sores are putrified and corrupted, because of my foolishness. I am become miserable, and am bowed down even to the end: I walked sorrowful all the day long. For my loins are filled with illusions; and there is no health in my flesh. I am afflicted and humbled exceedingly: I roared with the groaning of my heart. LORD, all my desire is before thee, and my groaning is not hidden from thee. My heart is troubled, my strength hath left me, and the light of my eyes itself is not with me. My friends and my neighbours have drawn near, and stood against me. And they that were near me stood afar off: And they that sought my soul used violence. And they that sought evils to me spoke vain things, and studied deceits all the day long. But I, as a deaf man, heard not: and as a dumb man not opening his mouth. And I became as a man that heareth not: and that hath no reproofs in his mouth. For in thee, O LORD, have I hoped: thou wilt hear me, O LORD my God. For I said: Lest at any time my enemies rejoice over me: and whilst my feet are moved, they speak great things against me. For I am ready for scourges: and my sorrow is continually before me. For I will declare my iniquity: and I will think for my sin. But my enemies live, and are stronger than I: and they that hate me wrongfully are multiplied. They that render evil for good, have detracted me, because I followed goodness. Forsake me not, O LORD my God: do not thou depart from me. Attend unto my help, O LORD, the God of my salvation.

38

Dixi custodiam

I said: I will take heed to my ways: that I sin not with my tongue. I have set guard to my mouth, when the sinner stood against me. I was dumb, and was humbled, and kept silence from good things: and my sorrow was renewed. My heart grew hot within me: and in my meditation a fire shall flame out. I spoke with my tongue: O LORD, make me know my end. And what is the number of my days: that I may know what is wanting to me. Behold thou hast made my days measurable: and my substance is as nothing before thee. And indeed all things are vanity: every man living. Surely man passeth as an image: yea, and he is disquieted in vain. He storeth up: and he knoweth not for whom he shall gather these things. And now what is my hope? is it not the LORD? and my substance is with thee. Deliver thou me from all my iniquities: thou hast made me a reproach to the fool. I was dumb, and I opened not my mouth, because thou hast done it. Remove thy scourges from me. The strength of thy hand hath made me faint in rebukes: Thou hast corrected man for iniquity. And thou hast made his soul to waste away like a spider: surely in vain is any man disquieted. Hear my prayer, O LORD, and my supplication: give ear to my tears. Be not silent: for I am a stranger with thee, and a sojourner as all my fathers were. O forgive me, that I may be refreshed, before I go hence, and be no more.

39

Expectans expectavi

With expectation I have waited for the LORD, and he was attentive to me. And he heard my prayers, and brought me out of the pit of misery and the mire of dregs. And he set my feet upon a rock, and directed my steps. And he put a new canticle into my mouth, a song to our God. Many shall see, and shall fear: and they shall hope in the LORD. Blessed is the man whose trust is in the name of the LORD; and who hath not had regard to vanities, and lying follies. Thou hast multiplied thy wonderful works, O LORD my God: and in thy thoughts there is no one like to thee. I have declared and I have spoken they are multiplied above number. Sacrifice and oblation thou didst not desire; but thou hast pierced ears for me. Burnt offering and sin offering thou didst not require: Then said I, Behold I come. In the head of the book it is written of me That I should do thy will: O my God, I have desired it, and thy law in the midst of my heart. I have declared thy justice in a great church, lo, I will not restrain my lips: O LORD, thou knowest it. I have not hid thy justice within my heart: I have declared thy truth and thy salvation. I have not concealed thy mercy and thy truth from a great council. Withhold not thou, O LORD, thy tender mercies from me: thy mercy and thy truth have always upheld me. For evils without number have surrounded me; my iniquities have overtaken me, and I was not able to see. They are multiplied above the hairs of my head: and my heart hath forsaken me. Be pleased, O LORD, to deliver me, look down, O LORD, to help me. Let them be confounded and ashamed together, that seek after my soul to take it away. Let them be turned backward and be ashamed that desire evils to me. Let them immediately bear their confusion, that say to me: Tis well, tis well. Let all that seek thee rejoice and be glad in thee: and let such as love thy salvation say always: The LORD be magnified. But I am a beggar and poor: the LORD is careful for me. Thou art my helper and my protector: O my God, be not slack.

40

Beatus qui intelligit

Blessed is he that understandeth concerning the needy and the poor: the LORD will deliver him in the evil day. The LORD preserve him and give him life, and make him blessed upon the earth: and deliver him not up to the will of his enemies. The LORD help him on his bed of sorrow: thou hast turned all his couch in his sickness. I said: O LORD, be thou merciful to me: heal my soul, for I have sinned against thee. My enemies have spoken evils against me: when shall he die and his name perish? And if he came in to see me, he spoke vain things: his heart gathered together iniquity to itself. He went out and spoke to the same purpose. All my enemies whispered together against me: they devised evils to me. They determined against me an unjust word: shall he that sleepeth rise again no more? For even the man of peace, in whom I trusted, who ate my bread, hath greatly supplanted me. But thou, O LORD, have mercy on me, and raise me up again: and I will requite them. By this I know, that thou hast had a good will for me: because my enemy shall not rejoice over me. But thou hast upheld me by reason of my innocence: and hast established me in thy sight forever. Blessed be the LORD the God of Israel from eternity to eternity. So be it. So be it.

41

Quemadmodum desiderat

As the hart panteth after the fountains of water; so my soul panteth after thee, O God. My soul hath thirsted after the strong living God; when shall I come and appear before the face of God? My tears have been my bread day and night, whilst it is said to me daily: Where is thy God? These things I remembered, and poured out my soul in me: for I shall go over into the place of the wonderful tabernacle, even to the house of God: With the voice of joy and praise; the noise of one feasting. Why art thou sad, O my soul? and why dost thou trouble me? Hope in God, for I will still give praise to him: the salvation of my countenance, And my God. My soul is troubled within myself: therefore will I remember thee from the land of Jordan and Hermoniim, from the little hill. Deep calleth on deep, at the noise of thy flood-gates. All thy heights and thy billows have passed over me. In the daytime the LORD hath commanded his mercy; and a canticle to him in the night. With me is prayer to the God of my life. I will say to God: Thou art my support. Why hast thou forgotten me? and why go I mourning, whilst my enemy afflicteth me? Whilst my bones are broken, my enemies who trouble me have reproached me; Whilst they say to me day by day: Where is thy God? Why art thou cast down, O my soul? and why dost thou disquiet me? Hope thou in God, for I will still give praise to him: the salvation of my countenance, and my God.

42

Judica me, Deus

Judge me, O God, and distinguish my cause from the nation that is not holy: deliver me from the unjust and deceitful man. For thou art God my strength: why hast thou cast me off? and why do I go sorrowful whilst the enemy afflicteth me? Send forth thy light and thy truth: they have conducted me, and brought me unto thy holy hill, and into thy tabernacles. And I will go in to the altar of God: to God who giveth joy to my youth. To thee, O God my God, I will give praise upon the harp: why art thou sad, O my soul? and why dost thou disquiet me? Hope in God, for I will still give praise to him: the salvation of my countenance, and my God.

43

Deus auribus nostris

We have heard, O God, with our ears: our fathers have declared to us, The work, thou hast wrought in their days, and in the days of old. Thy hand destroyed the Gentiles, and thou plantedst them: thou didst afflict the people and cast them out. For they got not the possession of the land by their own sword: neither did their own arm save them. But thy right hand and thy arm, and the light of thy countenance: because thou wast pleased with them. Thou art thyself my king and my God, who commandest the saving of Jacob. Through thee we will push down our enemies with the horn: and through thy name we will despise them that rise up against us. For I will not trust in my bow: neither shall my sword save me. But thou hast saved us from them that afflict us: and hast put them to shame that hate us. In God shall we glory all the day long: and in thy name we will give praise forever. But now thou hast cast us off, and put us to shame: and thou, O God, wilt not go out with our armies. Thou hast made us turn our back to our enemies: and they that hated us plundered for themselves. Thou hast given us up like sheep to be eaten: thou hast scattered us among the nations. Thou hast sold thy people for no price: and there was no reckoning in the exchange of them. Thou hast made us a reproach to our neighbours, a scoff and derision to them that are round about us. Thou hast made us a byword among the Gentiles: a shaking of the head among the people. All the day long my shame is before me: and the confusion of my face hath covered me, at the voice of him that reproacheth and detracteth me: at the face of the enemy and persecutor. All these things have come upon us, yet we have not forgotten thee: and we have not done wickedly in thy covenant. And our heart hath not turned back: neither hast thou turned aside our steps from thy way. For thou hast humbled us in the place of affliction: and the shadow of death hath covered us. If we have forgotten the name of our God, and if we have spread forth our hands to a strange god: Shall not God search out these things: for he knoweth the secrets of the heart. Because for thy sake we are killed all the day long: we are counted as sheep for the slaughter. Arise, why sleepest thou, O LORD? arise, and cast us not off to the end. Why turnest thou thy face away? and forgettest our want and our trouble? For our soul is humbled down to the dust: our belly cleaveth to the earth.

44

Eructavit cor meum

My heart hath uttered a good word: I speak my works to the king; My tongue is the pen of a scrivener that writeth swiftly. Thou art beautiful above the sons of men: grace is poured abroad in thy lips; therefore hath God blessed thee forever. Gird thy sword upon thy thigh, O thou most mighty. With thy comeliness and thy beauty set out, proceed prosperously, and reign. Because of truth and meekness and justice: and thy right hand shall conduct thee wonderfully. Thy arrows are sharp: under thee shall people fall, into the hearts of the king's enemies. Thy throne, O God, is for ever and ever: the sceptre of thy kingdom is a sceptre of uprightness. Thou hast loved justice, and hated iniquity: therefore God, thy God, hath anointed thee with the oil of gladness above thy fellows. Myrrh and stacte and cassia perfume thy garments, from the ivory houses: out of which the daughters of kings have delighted thee in thy glory. The queen stood on thy right hand, in gilded clothing; surrounded with variety. Hearken, O daughter, and see, and incline thy ear: and forget thy people and thy father's house. And the king shall greatly desire thy beauty; for he is the LORD thy God, and him they shall adore. And the daughters of Tyre with gifts, yea, all the rich among the people, shall entreat thy countenance. All the glory of the king's daughter is within in golden borders, clothed round about with varieties. After her shall virgins be brought to the king: her neighbours shall be brought to thee. They shall be brought with gladness and rejoicing: they shall be brought into the temple of the king. Instead of thy fathers, sons are born to thee: thou shalt make them princes over all the earth. They shall remember thy name throughout all generations. Therefore shall people praise thee forever; yea, forever and ever.

45

Deus noster refugium

Our God is our refuge and strength: a helper in troubles, which have found us exceedingly. Therefore we will not fear, when the earth shall be troubled; and the mountains shall be removed into the heart of the sea. Their waters roared and were troubled: the mountains were troubled with his strength. The stream of the river maketh the city of God joyful: the

Most High hath sanctified his own tabernacle. God is in the midst thereof, it shall not be moved: God will help it in the morning early. Nations were troubled, and kingdoms were bowed down: he uttered his voice, the earth trembled. The LORD of armies is with us: the God of Jacob is our protector. Come and behold ye the works of the LORD: what wonders he hath done upon earth, making wars to cease even to the end of the earth. He shall destroy the bow, and break the weapons: and the shield he shall burn in the fire. Be still and see that I am God; I will be exalted among the nations, and I will be exalted in the earth. The LORD of armies is with us: the God of Jacob is our protector.

47

Magnus Dominus

Great is the LORD, and exceedingly to be praised in the city of our God, in his holy mountain. With the joy of the whole earth is mount Zion founded, on the sides of the north, the city of the great king. In her houses shall God be known, when he shall protect her. For behold the kings of the earth assembled themselves: they gathered together. So they saw, and they wondered, they were troubled, they were moved: Trembling took hold of them. There were pains as of a woman in labour. With a vehement wind thou shalt break in pieces the ships of Tharsis. As we have heard, so have we seen, in the city of the LORD of hosts, in the city of our God: God hath founded it forever. We have received thy mercy, O God, in the midst of thy temple. According to thy name, O God, so also is thy praise unto the ends of the earth: thy right hand is full of justice. Let mount Zion rejoice, and the daughters of Judah be glad; because of thy judgments, O LORD. Surround Zion, and encompass her: tell ye in her towers. Set your hearts on her strength; and distribute her houses, that ye may relate it in another generation. For this is God, our God unto eternity, and forever and ever: he shall rule us forevermore.

48

Audite haec, omnes gentes

Hear these things, all ye nations: give ear, all ye inhabitants of the world. All you that are earthborn, and you sons of men: both rich and poor together. My mouth shall speak wisdom: and the meditation of my heart understanding. I will incline my ear to a parable; I will open my proposition on the psaltery. Why shall I fear in the evil day? the iniquity of my heel shall encompass me. They that trust in their own strength, and glory in the multitude of their riches, no brother can redeem, nor shall man redeem: he shall not give to God his ransom, nor the price of the redemption of his soul: and shall labour forever, and shall still live unto the end. He shall not see destruction, when he shall see the wise dying: the senseless and the fool shall perish together: And they shall leave their riches to strangers: And their sepulchres shall be their houses forever. Their dwelling places to all generations: they have called their lands by their names. And man when he was in honour did not understand; he is compared to senseless beasts, and is become like to them. This way of theirs is a stumbling block to them: and afterwards they shall delight in their mouth. They are laid in hell like sheep: death shall feed upon them. And the just shall have dominion over them in the morning; and their help shall decay in hell from their glory. But God will redeem my soul from the hand of hell, when he shall receive me. Be not thou afraid, when a man shall be made rich, and when the glory of his house shall be increased. For when he shall die he shall take nothing away; nor shall his glory descend with him. For in his lifetime his soul will be blessed: and he will praise thee when thou shalt do well to him. He shall go in to the generations of his fathers: and he shall never see light. Man when he was in honour did not understand: he hath been compared to senseless beasts, and made like to them.

49

Deus deorum

The God of gods, the LORD hath spoken: and he hath called the earth. From the rising of the sun, to the going down thereof: Out of Zion the loveliness of his beauty. God shall come manifestly: our God shall come, and shall not keep silence. A fire shall burn before him: and a mighty tempest shall be round about him. He shall call heaven from above, and the earth, to judge his people. Gather ye together his saints to him: who set his covenant before sacrifices. And the heavens shall declare his justice: for God is judge. Hear, O my people, and I will speak: O Israel, and I will testify to thee: I am God, thy God. I will not reprove thee for thy sacrifices: and thy burnt offerings are always in my sight. I will not take calves out of thy house: nor he goats out of thy flocks. For all the beasts of the woods are mine: the cattle on the hills, and the oxen. I know all the fowls of the air: and with me is the beauty of the field. If I should be hungry, I would not tell thee: for the world is mine, and the fulness thereof. Shall I eat the flesh of bullocks? or shall I drink the blood of goats? Offer to God the sacrifice of praise: and pay thy vows to the Most High. And call upon me in the day of trouble: I will deliver thee, and thou shalt glorify me. But to the sinner God hath said: Why dost thou declare my justices, and take my covenant in thy mouth? Seeing thou hast hated discipline: and hast cast my words behind thee. If thou didst see a thief thou didst run with him: and with adulterers thou hast been a partaker. Thy mouth hath abounded with evil, and thy tongue framed deceits. Sitting thou didst speak against thy brother, and didst lay a scandal against thy mother's son: These things hast thou done, and I was silent. Thou thoughtest unjustly that I should be like to thee: but I will reprove thee, and set before thy face. Understand these things, you that forget God; lest he snatch you away, and there be none to deliver you. The sacrifice of praise shall glorify me: and there is the way by which I will shew him the salvation of God.

Session Five

51

Quid gloriaris

Why dost thou glory in malice, thou that art mighty in iniquity? All the day long thy tongue hath devised injustice: as a sharp razor, thou hast wrought deceit. Thou hast loved malice more than goodness: and iniquity rather than to speak righteousness. Thou hast loved all the words of ruin, O deceitful tongue. Therefore will God destroy thee forever: he will pluck thee out, and remove thee from thy dwelling place: and thy root out of the land of the living. The just shall see and fear, and shall laugh at him, and say: Behold the man that made not God his helper: But trusted in the abundance of his riches: and prevailed in his vanity. But I, as a fruitful olive tree in the house of God, have hoped in the mercy of God for ever, yea for ever and ever. I will praise thee forever, because thou hast done it: and I will wait on thy name, for it is good in the sight of thy saints.

52

Dixit insipiens

The fool said in his heart: There is no God. They are corrupted, and become abominable in iniquities: there is none that doth good. God looked down from heaven on the children of men: to see if there were any that did understand, or did seek God. All have gone aside, they are become unprofitable together, there is none that doth good, no not one. Shall not all the workers of iniquity know, who eat up my people as they eat bread? They have not called upon God: there have they trembled for fear, where there was no fear. For God hath scattered the bones of them that please men: they have been confounded, because God hath despised them. Who will give out of Zion the salvation of Israel? when God shall bring back the captivity of his people, Jacob shall rejoice, and Israel shall be glad.

54

Exaudi, Deus

Hear, O God, my prayer, and despise not my supplication: Be attentive to me and hear me. I am grieved in my exercise; and am troubled, At the voice of the enemy, and at the tribulation of the sinner. For they have cast iniquities upon me: and in wrath they were troublesome to me. My heart is troubled within me: and the fear of death is fallen upon me. Fear and trembling are come upon me: and darkness hath covered me. And I said: Who will give me wings like a dove, and I will fly and be at rest? Lo, I have gone far off flying away; and I abode in the wilderness. I waited for him that hath saved me from pusillanimity of spirit, and a storm. Cast down, O LORD, and divide their tongues; for I have seen iniquity and contradiction in the city. Day and night shall iniquity surround it upon its walls: and in the midst thereof are labour, and injustice. And usury and deceit have not departed from its streets. For if my enemy had reviled me, I would verily have borne with it. And if he that hated me had spoken great things against me, I would perhaps have hidden myself from him. But thou a man of one mind, my guide, and my familiar, who didst take sweetmeats together with me: in the house of God we walked with consent. Let death come upon them, and let them go down alive into hell. For there is wickedness in their dwellings: in the midst of them. But I have cried to God: and the LORD will save me. Evening and morning, and at noon I will speak and declare: and he shall hear my voice. He shall redeem my soul in peace from them that draw near to me: for among many they were with me. God shall hear, and the Eternal shall humble them. For there is no change with them, and they have not feared God: He hath stretched forth his hand to repay. They have defiled his covenant, they are divided by the wrath of his countenance, and his heart hath drawn near. His words are smoother than oil, and the same are darts. Cast thy care upon the LORD, and he shall sustain thee: he shall not suffer the just to waver forever. But thou, O God, shalt bring them down into the pit of destruction. Bloody and deceitful men shall not live out half their days; but I will trust in thee, O LORD.

55

Miserere mei, Deus

Have mercy on me, O God, for man hath trodden me under foot; all the day long he hath afflicted me fighting against me. My enemies have trodden on me all the day long; for they are many that make war against me. From the height of the day I shall fear: but I will trust in thee. In God I will praise my words, in God I have put my trust: I will not fear what flesh can do against me. All the day long they detested my words: all their thoughts were against me unto evil. They will dwell and hide themselves: they will watch my heel. As they have waited for my soul, for nothing shalt thou save them: in thy anger thou shalt break the people in pieces, O God, I have declared to thee my life: thou hast set my tears in thy sight, as also in thy promise. Then shall my enemies be turned back. In what day soever I shall call upon thee, behold I know thou art my God. In God will I praise the word, in the LORD will I praise his speech. In God have I hoped, I will not fear what man can do to me. In me, O God, are vows to thee, which I will pay, praises to thee: Because thou hast delivered my soul from death, my feet from falling: that I may please in the sight of God, in the light of the living.

56

Miserere mei, Deus

Have mercy on me, O God, have mercy on me: for my soul trusteth in thee. And in the shadow of thy wings will I hope, until iniquity pass away. I will cry to God the Most High; to God who hath done good to me. He hath sent from heaven and delivered me: he hath made them a reproach that trod upon me. God hath sent his mercy and his truth, and he hath delivered my soul from the midst of the young lions. I slept troubled. The sons of men, whose teeth are weapons and arrows, and their tongue a sharp sword. Be thou exalted, O God, above the heavens, and thy glory above all the earth. They prepared a snare for my feet; and they bowed down my soul. They dug a pit before my face, and they are fallen into it. My heart is ready, O God, my heart is ready: I will Sing, and rehearse a psalm. Arise, O my glory, arise psaltery and harp: I will arise early. I will give praise to thee, O LORD, among the people: I will sing a psalm to thee among the nations. For thy mercy is magnified even to the heavens: and thy truth unto the clouds. Be thou exalted, O God, above the heavens: and thy glory above all the earth.

57

Si vere utique

If in very deed you speak justice: judge right things, ye sons of men. For in your heart you work iniquity: your hands forge injustice in the earth. The wicked are alienated from the womb; they have gone astray from the womb: they have spoken false things. Their madness is according to the likeness of a serpent: like the deaf asp that stoppeth her ears: Which will not hear the voice of the charmers; nor of the wizard that charmeth wisely. God shall break in pieces their teeth in their mouth: the LORD shall break the grinders of the lions. They shall come to nothing, like water running down; he hath bent his bow till they be weakened. Like wax that melteth they shall be taken away: fire hath fallen on them, and they shall not see the sun. Before your thorns could know the brier; he swalloweth them up, as alive, in his wrath. The just shall rejoice when he shall see the revenge: he shall wash his hands in the blood of the sinner. And man shall say: If indeed there be fruit to the just: there is indeed a God that judgeth them on the earth.

58

Eripe me

Deliver me from my enemies, O my God; and defend me from them that
rise up against me. Deliver me from them that work iniquity, and save me
from bloody men. For behold they have caught my soul: the mighty have
rushed in upon me: Neither is it my iniquity, nor my sin, O LORD: without
iniquity have I run, and directed my steps. Rise up thou to meet me, and
behold: even thou, O LORD, the God of hosts, the God of Israel. Attend
to visit all the nations: have no mercy on all them that work iniquity. They
shall return at evening, and shall suffer hunger like dogs: and shall go round
about the city. Behold they shall speak with their mouth, and a sword is in
their lips: for who, say they, hath heard us? But thou, O LORD, shalt laugh
at them: thou shalt bring all the nations to nothing. I will keep my strength
to thee: for thou art my protector: My God, his mercy shall prevent me.
God shall let me see over my enemies: slay them not, lest at any time my
people forget. Scatter them by thy power; and bring them down, O LORD,
my protector: For the sin of their mouth, and the word of their lips: and let
them be taken in their pride. And for their cursing and lying they shall be
talked of, when they are consumed: when they are consumed by thy wrath,
and they shall be no more. And they shall know that God will rule Jacob,
and all the ends of the earth. They shall return at evening and shall suffer
hunger like dogs: and shall go round about the city. They shall be scattered
abroad to eat, and shall murmur if they be not filled. But I will sing thy
strength: and will extol thy mercy in the morning. For thou art become my
support, and my refuge, in the day of my trouble. Unto thee, O my helper,
will I sing, for thou art God my defence: my God my mercy.

59

Deus, repulisti nos

O God, thou hast cast us off, and hast destroyed us; thou hast been angry,
and hast had mercy on us. Thou hast moved the earth, and hast troubled
it: heal thou the breaches thereof, for it has been moved. Thou hast shewn
thy people hard things; thou hast made us drink wine of sorrow. Thou
hast given a warning to them that fear thee: that they may flee from before
the bow: That thy beloved may be delivered. Save me with thy right hand,

and hear me. God hath spoken in his holy place: I will rejoice, and I will divide Sichem; and will mete out the vale of tabernacles. Galaad is mine, and Manasses is mine: and Ephraim is the strength of my head. Judah is my king: Moab is the pot of my hope. Into Edom will I stretch out my shoe: to me the foreigners are made subject. Who will bring me into the strong city? Who will lead me into Edom? Wilt not thou, O God, who hast cast us off? And wilt not thou, O God, go out with our armies? Give us help from trouble: for vain is the salvation of man. Through God we shall do mightily: and he shall bring to nothing them that afflict us.

60

Exaudi, Deus

Hear, O God, my supplication: be attentive to my prayer, to thee have I cried from the ends of the earth: when my heart was in anguish, thou hast exalted me on a rock. Thou hast conducted me; For thou hast been my hope; a tower of strength against the face of the enemy. In thy tabernacle I shall dwell forever: I shall be protected under the covert of thy wings. For thou, my God, hast heard my prayer: thou hast given an inheritance to them that fear thy name. Thou wilt add days to the days of the king: his years even to generation and generation. He abideth forever in the sight of God: his mercy and truth who shall search? So will I sing a psalm to thy name for ever and ever: that I may pay my vows from day to day.

61

Nonne Deo

Shall not my soul be subject to God? for from him is my salvation. For he is my God and my saviour: he is my protector, I shall be moved no more. How long do you rush in upon a man? you all kill, as if you were thrusting down a leaning wall, and a tottering fence. But they have thought to cast away my price; I ran in thirst: they blessed with their mouth, but cursed with their heart. But be thou, O my soul, subject to God: for from him is my patience. For he is my God and my saviour: he is my helper, I shall not be moved. In God is my salvation and my glory: he is the God of my help, and my hope is in God. Trust in him, all ye congregation of people: pour out your hearts before him. God is our helper forever. But vain are the sons of men, the sons of men are liars in the balances: that by vanity they may together deceive. Trust not in iniquity, and cover not robberies: if riches abound, set not your heart upon them. God hath spoken once, these two things have I heard, that power belongeth to God, and mercy to thee, O LORD; for thou wilt render to every man according to his works.

63

Exaudi Deus orationem

Hear, O God, my prayer, when I make supplication to thee: deliver my soul from the fear of the enemy. Thou hast protected me from the assembly of the malignant; from the multitude of the workers of iniquity. For they have whetted their tongues like a sword; they have bent their bow a bitter thing, to shoot in secret the undefiled. They will shoot at him on a sudden, and will not fear: they are resolute in wickedness. They have talked of hiding snares; they have said: Who shall see them? They have searched after iniquities: they have failed in their search. Man shall come to a deep heart: And God shall be exalted. The arrows of children are their wounds: And their tongues against them are made weak. All that saw them were troubled; And every man was afraid. And they declared the works of God: and understood his doings. The just shall rejoice in the LORD, and shall hope in him: and all the upright in heart shall be praised.

65

Jubilate Deo

Shout with joy to God, all the earth, sing ye a psalm to his name; give glory to his praise. Say unto God, How terrible are thy works, O LORD! in the multitude of thy strength thy enemies shall lie to thee. Let all the earth adore thee, and sing to thee: let it sing a psalm to thy name. Come and see the works of God; who is terrible in his counsels over the sons of men. Who turneth the sea into dry land, in the river they shall pass on foot: there shall we rejoice in him. Who by his power ruleth for ever: his eyes behold the nations; let not them that provoke him be exalted in themselves. O bless our God, ye Gentiles: and make the voice of his praise to be heard. Who hath set my soul to live: and hath not suffered my feet to be moved: For thou, O God, hast proved us: thou hast tried us by fire, as silver is tried. Thou hast brought us into a net, thou hast laid afflictions on our back: Thou hast set men over our heads. We have passed through fire and water, and thou hast brought us out into a refreshment. I will go into thy house with burnt offerings: I will pay thee my vows, which my lips have uttered, and my mouth hath spoken, when I was in trouble. I will offer up to thee holocausts full of marrow, with burnt offerings of rams: I will offer to thee bullocks with goats. Come and hear, all ye that fear God, and I will tell you what great things he hath done for my soul. I cried to him with my mouth: and I extolled him with my tongue. If I have looked at iniquity in my heart, the LORD will not hear me. Therefore hath God heard me, and hath attended to the voice of my supplication. Blessed be God, who hath not turned away my prayer, nor his mercy from me.

Session Six

67

Exurgat Deus

Let God arise, and let his enemies be scattered: and let them that hate him flee from before his face. As smoke vanisheth, so let them vanish away: as wax melteth before the fire, so let the wicked perish at the presence of God. And let the just feast, and rejoice before God: and be delighted with glad-ness. Sing ye to God, sing a psalm to his name, make a way for him who ascendeth upon the west: the LORD is his name. Rejoice ye before him: but the wicked shall be troubled at his presence, who is the father of orphans, and the judge of widows. God in his holy place: God who maketh men of one manner to dwell in a house: Who bringeth out them that were bound in strength; in like manner them that provoke, that dwell in sepulchres. O God, when thou didst go forth in the sight of thy people, when thou didst pass through the desert: The earth was moved, and the heavens dropped at the presence of the God of Sina, at the presence of the God of Israel. Thou shalt set aside for thy inheritance a free rain, O God: and it was weakened, but thou hast made it perfect. In it shall thy animals dwell; in thy sweetness, O God, thou hast provided for the poor. The LORD shall give the word to them that preach good tidings with great power. The king of powers is of the beloved, of the beloved; and the beauty of the house shall divide spoils.

If you sleep among the midst of lots, you shall be as the wings of a dove covered with silver, and the hinder parts of her back with the paleness of gold. When he that is in heaven appointeth kings over her, they shall be whited with snow in Selmon. The mountain of God is a fat mountain. A curdled mountain, a fat mountain. Why suspect, ye curdled mountains? A mountain in which God is well pleased to dwell: for there the LORD shall dwell unto the end. The chariot of God is attended by ten thousands; thousands of them that rejoice: the LORD is among them in Sina, in the holy place. Thou hast ascended on high, thou hast led captivity captive; thou hast received gifts in men. Yea for those also that do not believe, the dwelling of the LORD God. Blessed be the LORD day by day: the God of our salvation will make our journey prosperous to us. Our God is the God of salvation: and of the LORD, of the LORD are the issues from death. But God shall break the heads of his enemies: the hairy crown of them that walk on in their sins. The LORD said: I will turn them from Basan, I will turn them into the depth of the sea: That thy foot may be dipped in the blood of thy enemies; the tongue of thy dogs be red with the same. They have seen thy goings, O God, the goings of my God: of my king who is in his sanctuary. Princes went before joined with singers, in the midst of young damsels playing on timbrels. In the churches bless ye God the LORD, from the fountains of Israel. There is Benjamin a youth, in ecstasy of mind. The princes of Juda are their leaders: the princes of Zabulon, the princes of Nephthali. Command thy strength, O God: confirm, O God, what thou hast wrought in us. From thy temple in Jerusalem, kings shall offer presents to thee. Rebuke the wild beasts of the reeds, the congregation of bulls with the kine of the people; who seek to exclude them who are tried with silver. Scatter thou the nations that delight in wars: Ambassadors shall come out of Egypt: Ethiopia shall soon stretch out her hands to God. Sing to God, ye kingdoms of the earth: sing ye to the LORD: Sing ye to God, who mounteth above the heaven of heavens, to the east. Behold he will give to his voice the voice of power: Give ye glory to God for Israel, his magnificence, and his power is in the clouds. God is wonderful in his saints: the God of Israel is he who will give power and strength to his people. Blessed be God.

68

Salvum me fac, Deus

Save me, O God: for the waters are come in even unto my soul. I stick fast in the mire of the deep: and there is no sure standing. I am come into the depth of the sea: and a tempest hath overwhelmed me. I have laboured with crying; my jaws are become hoarse: my eyes have failed, whilst I hope in my God. They are multiplied above the hairs of my head, who hate me without cause. My enemies are grown strong who have wrongfully persecuted me: then did I pay that which I took not away. O God, thou knowest my foolishness; and my offences are not hidden from thee: Let not them be ashamed for me, who look for thee, O LORD, the LORD of hosts. Let them not be confounded on my account, who seek thee, O God of Israel. Because for thy sake I have borne reproach; shame hath covered my face. I am become a stranger to my brethren, and an alien to the sons of my mother. For the zeal of thy house hath eaten me up: and the reproaches of them that reproached thee are fallen upon me. And I covered my soul in fasting: and it was made a reproach to me. And I made haircloth my garment: and I became a byword to them. They that sat in the gate spoke against me: and they that drank wine made me their song. But as for me, my prayer is to thee, O LORD; for the time of thy good pleasure, O God. In the multitude of thy mercy hear me, in the truth of thy salvation. Draw me out of the mire, that I may not stick fast: deliver me from them that hate me, and out of the deep waters. Let not the tempest of water drown me, nor the deep swallow me up: and let not the pit shut her mouth upon me. Hear me, O LORD, for thy mercy is kind; look upon me according to the multitude of thy tender mercies. And turn not away thy face from thy servant: for I am in trouble, hear me speedily. Attend to my soul, and deliver it: save me because of my enemies. Thou knowest my reproach, and my confusion, and my shame. In thy sight are all they that afflict me; my heart hath expected reproach and misery. And I looked for one that would grieve together with me, but there was none: and for one that would comfort me, and I found none. And they gave me gall for my food, and in my thirst they gave me vinegar to drink. Let their table become as a snare before them, and a recompense, and a stumbling block. Let their eyes be darkened that they see not; and their back bend thou down always. Pour out thy indignation upon them: and let thy wrathful anger take hold of them. Let their habitation be made desolate: and let there be none to dwell in their tabernacles. Because they have persecuted him whom thou hast smitten; and they have added to the grief of my wounds. Add thou iniquity upon their iniquity: and let them not come into thy justice. Let them be blotted out of the book of the living; and with the just let them not be written. But I am poor and sorrowful: thy salvation, O God, hath set me up. I will praise the name of God with a canticle: and I will magnify him with praise. And it shall please God better than a young calf, that bringeth forth horns and hoofs. Let the poor see and rejoice: seek ye God, and your soul shall live. For the LORD hath heard the poor: and hath not despised his prisoners. Let the heavens and the earth praise him; the sea, and everything that creepeth therein. For God will save Zion, and the cities of Judah shall be built up. And they shall dwell there, and acquire it by inheritance. And the seed of his servants shall possess it; and they that love his name shall dwell therein.

70

In te, Domine

In thee, O LORD, I have hoped, let me never be put to confusion: Deliver me in thy justice, and rescue me. Incline thy ear unto me, and save me. Be thou unto me a God, a protector, and a place of strength: that thou mayst make me safe. For thou art my firmament and my refuge. Deliver me, O my God, out of the hand of the sinner, and out of the hand of the transgressor of the law and of the unjust. For thou art my patience, O LORD: my hope, O LORD, from my youth; By thee have I been confirmed from the womb: from my mother's womb thou art my protector. Of thee shall I continually sing: I am become unto many as a wonder, but thou art a strong helper. Let my mouth be filled with praise, that I may sing thy glory; thy greatness all the day long. Cast me not off in the time of old age: when my strength shall fail, do not thou forsake me. For my enemies have spoken against me; and they that watched my soul have consulted together, saying: God hath forsaken him: pursue and take him, for there is none to deliver him. O God, be not thou far from me: O my God, make haste to my help. Let them be confounded and come to nothing that detract my soul; let them be covered with confusion and shame that seek my hurt. But I will always hope; and will add to all thy praise. My mouth shall shew forth thy justice; thy salvation all the day long. Because I have not known learning, I will enter into the powers of the LORD: O LORD, I will be mindful of thy justice alone.

Thou hast taught me, O God, from my youth: and till now I will declare thy wonderful works. And unto old age and grey hairs: O God, forsake me not, Until I shew forth thy arm to all the generation that is to come: Thy power, and thy justice, O God, even to the highest great things thou hast done: O God, who is like to thee? How great troubles hast thou shewn me, many and grievous: and turning thou hast brought me to life, and hast brought me back again from the depths of the earth: Thou hast multiplied thy magnificence; and turning to me thou hast comforted me. For I will also confess to thee thy truth with the instruments of psaltery: O God, I will sing to thee with the harp, thou holy one of Israel. My lips shall greatly rejoice, when I shall sing to thee; and my soul which thou hast redeemed. Yea and my tongue shall meditate on thy justice all the day; when they shall be confounded and put to shame that seek evils to me.

71

Deus, judicium tuum

Give to the king thy judgment, O God: and to the king's son thy justice: To judge thy people with justice, and thy poor with judgment. Let the mountains receive peace for the people: and the hills justice. He shall judge the poor of the people, and he shall save the children of the poor: and he shall humble the oppressor. And he shall continue with the sun, and before the moon, throughout all generations. He shall come down like rain upon the fleece; and as showers falling gently upon the earth. In his days shall justice spring up, and abundance of peace, till the moon be taken away. And he shall rule from sea to sea, and from the river unto the ends of the earth. Before him the Ethiopians shall fall down: and his enemies shall lick the ground. The kings of Tharsis and the islands shall offer presents: the kings of the Arabians and of Saba shall bring gifts: And all kings of the earth shall adore him: all nations shall serve him. For he shall deliver the poor from the mighty: and the needy that had no helper. He shall spare the poor and needy: and he shall save the souls of the poor. He shall redeem their souls from usuries and iniquity: and their names shall be honourable in his sight. And he shall live, and to him shall be given of the gold of Arabia, for him they shall always adore: they shall bless him all the day. And there shall be a firmament on the earth on the tops of mountains, above Libanus shall the fruit thereof be exalted: and they of the city shall flourish like the grass of the earth. Let his name be blessed for evermore: his name continueth before the sun. And in him shall all the tribes of the earth be blessed: all nations shall magnify him. Blessed be the LORD, the God of Israel, who alone doth wonderful things. And blessed be the name of his majesty forever: and the whole earth shall be filled with his majesty. So be it. So be it. The praises of David, the son of Jesse, are ended.

72

Quam bonus Israel Deus

How good is God to Israel, to them that are of a right heart! But my feet were almost moved; my steps had well nigh slipped. Because I had a zeal on occasion of the wicked, seeing the prosperity of sinners. For there is no regard to their death, nor is there strength in their stripes. They are not in the labour of men: neither shall they be scourged like other men. Therefore pride hath held them fast: they are covered with their iniquity and their wickedness. Their iniquity hath come forth, as it were from fatness: they have passed into the affection of the heart. They have thought and spoken wickedness: they have spoken iniquity on high. They have set their mouth against heaven: and their tongue hath passed through the earth. Therefore will my people return here and full days shall be found in them. And they said: How doth God know? and is there knowledge in the Most High? Behold these are sinners; and yet abounding in the world they have obtained riches. And I said: Then have I in vain justified my heart, and washed my hands among the innocent. And I have been scourged all the day; and my chastisement hath been in the mornings. If I said: I will speak thus; behold I should condemn the generation of thy children. I studied that I might know this thing, it is a labour in my sight: Until I go into the sanctuary of God, and understand concerning their last ends. But indeed for deceits thou hast put it to them: when they were lifted up thou hast cast them down. How are they brought to desolation? they have suddenly ceased to be: they have perished by reason of their iniquity. As the dream of them that awake, O LORD; so in thy city thou shalt bring their image to nothing. For my heart hath been inflamed, and my reins have been changed: And I am brought to nothing, and I knew not. I am become as a beast before thee: and I am always with thee. Thou hast held me by my right hand; and by thy will thou hast conducted me, and with thy glory thou hast received me. For what have I in heaven? and besides thee what do I desire upon earth? For thee my flesh and my heart hath fainted away: thou art the God of my heart, and the God that is my portion forever. For behold they that go far from thee shall perish: thou hast destroyed all them that are disloyal to thee. But it is good for me to adhere to my God, to put my hope in the LORD God: That I may declare all thy praises, in the gates of the daughter of Zion.

73

Ut quid, Deus

O God, why hast thou cast us off unto the end: why is thy wrath enkindled against the sheep of thy pasture? Remember thy congregation, which thou hast possessed from the beginning. The sceptre of thy inheritance which thou hast redeemed: mount Zion in which thou hast dwelt. Lift up thy hands against their pride unto the end; see what things the enemy hath done wickedly in the sanctuary. And they that hate thee have made their boasts, in the midst of thy solemnity. They have set up their ensigns for signs, And they knew not both in the going out and on the highest top. As with axes in a wood of trees, They have cut down at once the gates thereof, with axe and hatchet they have brought it down. They have set fire to thy sanctuary: they have defiled the dwelling place of thy name on the earth. They said in their heart, the whole kindred of them together: Let us abolish all the festival days of God from the land. Our signs we have not seen, there is now no prophet: and he will know us no more. How long, O God, shall the enemy reproach: is the adversary to provoke thy name forever? Why dost thou turn away thy hand: and thy right hand out of the midst of thy bosom forever? But God is our king before ages: he hath wrought salvation in the midst of the earth. Thou by thy strength didst make the sea firm: thou didst crush the heads of the dragons in the waters. Thou hast broken the heads of the dragon: thou hast given him to be meat for the people of the Ethiopians. Thou hast broken up the fountains and the torrents: thou hast dried up the Ethan rivers. Thine is the day, and thine is the night: thou hast made the morning light and the sun. Thou hast made all the borders of the earth: the summer and the spring were formed by thee. Remember this, the enemy hath reproached the LORD: and a foolish people hath provoked thy name. Deliver not up to beasts the souls that confess to thee: and forget not to the end the souls of thy poor. Have regard to thy covenant: for they that are the obscure of the earth have been filled with dwellings of iniquity. Let not the humble be turned away with confusion: the poor and needy shall praise thy name. Arise, O God, judge thy own cause: remember thy reproaches with which the foolish man hath reproached thee all the day. Forget not the voices of thy enemies: the pride of them that hate thee ascendeth continually.

74

Confitebimur tibi

We will praise thee, O God: we will praise, and we will call upon thy name. We will relate thy wondrous works: When I shall take a time, I will judge justices. The earth is melted, and all that dwell therein: I have established the pillars thereof. I said to the wicked: Do not act wickedly: and to the sinners: Lift not up the horn. Lift not up your horn on high: speak not iniquity against God. For neither from the east, nor from the west, nor from the desert hills: For God is the judge. One he putteth down, and another he lifteth up: For in the hand of the LORD there is a cup of strong wine full of mixture. And he hath poured it out from this to that: but the dregs thereof are not emptied: all the sinners of the earth shall drink. But I will declare forever: I will sing to the God of Jacob. And I will break all the horns of sinners: but the horns of the just shall be exalted.

75

Notus in Judaea

In Judea God is known: his name is great in Israel. And his place is in peace: and his abode in Sion: There hath he broken the powers of bows, the shield, the sword, and the battle. Thou enlightenest wonderfully from the everlasting hills. All the foolish of heart were troubled. They have slept their sleep; and all the men of riches have found nothing in their hands. At thy rebuke, O God of Jacob, they have all slumbered that mounted on horseback. Thou art terrible, and who shall resist thee? from that time thy wrath. Thou hast caused judgment to be heard from heaven: the earth trembled and was still, When God arose in judgment, to save all the meek of the earth. For the thought of man shall give praise to thee: and the remainders of the thought shall keep holiday to thee. Vow ye, and pay to the LORD your God: all you that are round about him bring presents. To him that is terrible, even to him who taketh away the spirit of princes: to the terrible with the kings of the earth.

76

Voce mea

I cried to the LORD with my voice; to God with my voice, and he gave ear to me. In the day of my trouble I sought God, with my hands lifted up to him in the night, and I was not deceived. My soul refused to be comforted: I remembered God, and was delighted, and was exercised, and my spirit swooned away. My eyes prevented the watches: I was troubled, and I spoke not. I thought upon the days of old: and I had in my mind the eternal years. And I meditated in the night with my own heart: and I was exercised and I swept my spirit. Will God then cast off forever? or will he never be more favourable again? Or will he cut off his mercy forever, from generation to generation? Or will God forget to shew mercy? or will he in his anger shut up his mercies? And I said, Now have I begun: this is the change of the right hand of the Most High. I remembered the works of the LORD: for I will be mindful of thy wonders from the beginning. And I will meditate on all thy works: and will be employed in thy inventions. Thy way, O God, is in the holy place: who is the great God like our God? Thou art the God that dost wonders. Thou hast made thy power known among the nations: With thy arm thou hast redeemed thy people the children of Jacob and of Joseph. The waters saw thee, O God, the waters saw thee: and they were afraid, and the depths were troubled. Great was the noise of the waters: the clouds sent out a sound. For thy arrows pass: The voice of thy thunder in a wheel. Thy lightnings enlightened the world: the earth shook and trembled. Thy way is in the sea, and thy paths in many waters: and thy footsteps shall not be known. Thou hast conducted thy people like sheep, by the hand of Moses and Aaron.

77

Attendite

Attend, O my people, to my law: incline your ears to the words of my mouth. I will open my mouth in parables: I will utter propositions from the beginning. How great things have we heard and known, and our fathers have told us. They have not been hidden from their children, in another generation. Declaring the praises of the LORD, and his powers, and his wonders which he hath done. And he set up a testimony in Jacob: and made a law in Israel. How great things he commanded our fathers, that they should make the same known to their children: That another generation might know them. The children that should be born and should rise up, and declare them to their children. That they may put their hope in God and may not forget the works of God: and may seek his commandments. That they may not become like their fathers, a perverse and exasperating generation. A generation that set not their heart aright: and whose spirit was not faithful to God. The sons of Ephraim who bend and shoot with the bow: they have turned back in the day of battle. They kept not the covenant of God: and in his law they would not walk. And they forgot his benefits, and his wonders that he had shewn them. Wonderful things did he do in the sight of their fathers, in the land of Egypt, in the field of Tanis. He divided the sea and brought them through: and he made the waters to stand as in a vessel. And he conducted them with a cloud by day: and all the night with a light of fire. He struck the rock in the wilderness: and gave them to drink, as out of the great deep. He brought forth water out of the rock: and made streams run down as rivers. And they added yet more sin against him: they provoked the Most High to wrath in the place without water. And they tempted God in their hearts, by asking meat for their desires. And they spoke ill of God: they said: Can God furnish a table in the wilderness? Because he struck the rock, and the waters gushed out, and the streams overflowed. Can he also give bread, or provide a table for his people? Therefore the LORD heard, and was angry: and a fire was kindled against Jacob, and wrath came up against Israel. Because they believed not in God: and trusted not in his salvation. And he had commanded the clouds from above, and had opened the doors of heaven. And had rained down manna upon them to eat, and had given them the bread of heaven. Man ate the bread of angels: he sent them provisions in abundance. He removed the south wind from heaven: and by his power brought in the southwest wind. And he rained upon them flesh as dust: and feathered fowls like as the sand of the sea. And they fell in the midst of their camp, round about their pavilions. So they did eat, and were filled exceedingly, and he gave them their desire: They were not defrauded of that which they craved. As yet their meat was in their mouth: And the wrath of God came upon them. And he slew the fat ones amongst them, and brought down the chosen men of Israel. In all these things they sinned still: and they believed not for his wondrous works. And their days were consumed in vanity, and their years in haste. When he slew them, then they sought him: and they returned, and came to him early in the morning. And they remembered that God was their helper: and the Most High God their redeemer. And they loved him with their mouth: and with their tongue they lied unto him: But their heart was not right with him: nor were they counted faithful in his covenant. But he is merciful, and will forgive their sins: and will not destroy them. And many a time did he turn away his anger: and did not kindle all his wrath. And he remembered that they are flesh: a wind that goeth and returneth not. How often did they provoke him in the desert: and move him to wrath in the place without water? And they turned back and tempted God: and grieved the holy one of Israel. They remembered not his hand, in the day that he redeemed them from the hand of him that afflicted them: How he wrought his signs in Egypt, and his wonders in the field of Tanis. And he turned their rivers into blood, and their showers that they might not drink. He sent amongst them divers sores of flies, which devoured them: and frogs which destroyed them. And he gave up their fruits to the blast, and their labours to the locust. And he destroyed their vineyards with hail, and their mulberry trees with hoarfrost. And he gave up their cattle to the hail, and their stock to the fire. And he sent upon them the wrath of his indignation: indignation and wrath and trouble, which he sent by evil angels. He made a way for a path to his anger: he spared not their souls from death, and their cattle he shut up in death. And he killed all the firstborn in the land of Egypt: the firstfruits of all their labour in the tabernacles of Cham. And he took away his own people as sheep: and guided them in the wilderness like a flock. And he brought them out in hope, and they feared not: and the sea overwhelmed their enemies. And he brought them into the mountain of his sanctuary: the mountain which his right hand had purchased. And he cast out the Gentiles before them: and by lot divided to them their land by a line of distribution. And he made the tribes of Israel to dwell in their tabernacles. Yet they tempted, and provoked the Most High God: and they kept not his testimonies. And they turned away, and kept not the covenant: even like their fathers they were turned aside as a crooked bow. They provoked him to anger on their hills: and moved him to jealousy with their graven things. God heard, and despised them, and he reduced Israel exceedingly as it were to nothing. And he put away the tabernacle of Silo, his tabernacle where he dwelt among men. And he delivered their strength into captivity: and their beauty into the hands of the enemy. And he shut up his people under the sword: and he despised his inheritance. Fire consumed their young men: and their maidens were not lamented. Their priests fell by the sword: and their widows did not mourn. And the LORD was awaked as one out of sleep, and like a mighty man that hath been surfeited with wine. And he smote his enemies on the hinder parts: he put them to an everlasting reproach. And he rejected the tabernacle of Joseph: and chose not the tribe of Ephraim: But he chose the tribe of Juda, mount Zion which he loved. And he built his sanctuary as of unicorns, in the land which he founded forever. And he chose his servant David, and took him from the flocks of sheep: he brought him from following the ewes great with young, To feed Jacob his servant, and Israel his inheritance. And he fed them in the innocence of his heart: and conducted them by the skillfulness of his hands.

78

Deus, venerunt gentes

O God, the heathens are come into thy inheritance, they have defiled thy holy temple: they have made Jerusalem as a place to keep fruit. They have given the dead bodies of thy servants to be meat for the fowls of the air: the flesh of thy saints for the beasts of the earth. They have poured out their blood as water, round about Jerusalem and there was none to bury them. We are become a reproach to our neighbours: a scorn and derision to them that are round about us. How long, O LORD, wilt thou be angry forever: shall thy zeal be kindled like a fire? Pour out thy wrath upon the nations that have not known thee: and upon the kingdoms that have not called upon thy name. Because they have devoured Jacob; and have laid waste his place. Remember not our former iniquities: let thy mercies speedily prevent us, for we are become exceeding poor. Help us, O God, our saviour: and for the glory of thy name, O LORD, deliver us: and forgive us our sins for thy name's sake: Lest they should say among the Gentiles: Where is their God? And let him be made known among the nations before our eyes, By the revenging the blood of thy servants, which hath been shed: Let the sighing of the prisoners come in before thee. According to the greatness of thy arm, take possession of the children of them that have been put to death. And render to our neighbours sevenfold in their bosom: the reproach wherewith they have reproached thee, O LORD. But we thy people, and the sheep of thy pasture, will give thanks to thee forever. We will shew forth thy praise, unto generation and generation.

79

Qui regis Israel

Give ear, O thou that rulest Israel: thou that leadest Joseph like a sheep. Thou that sittest upon the cherubims, shine forth Before Ephraim, Benjamin, and Manasses. Stir up thy might, and come to save us. Convert us, O God: and shew us thy face, and we shall be saved. O LORD God of hosts, how long wilt thou be angry against the prayer of thy servant? How long wilt thou feed us with the bread of tears: and give us for our drink tears in measure? Thou hast made us to be a contradiction to our neighbours: and our enemies have scoffed at us. O God of hosts, convert us: and shew thy face, and we shall be saved. Thou hast brought a vineyard out of Egypt: thou hast cast out the Gentiles and planted it. Thou wast the guide of its journey in its sight: thou plantedst the roots thereof, and it filled the land. The shadow of it covered the hills: and the branches thereof the cedars of God. It stretched forth its branches unto the sea, and its boughs unto the river. Why hast thou broken down the hedge thereof, so that all they who pass by the way do pluck it? The boar out of the wood hath laid it waste: and a singular wild beast hath devoured it. Turn again, O God of hosts, look down from heaven, and see, and visit this vineyard: And perfect the same which thy right hand hath planted: and upon the son of man whom thou hast confirmed for thyself. Things set on fire and dug down shall perish at the rebuke of thy countenance. Let thy hand be upon the man of thy right hand: and upon the son of man whom thou hast confirmed for thyself. And we depart not from thee, thou shalt quicken us: and we will call upon thy name. O LORD God of hosts, convert us: and shew thy face, and we shall be saved.

Session Seven

80

Exultate Deo

Rejoice to God our helper: sing aloud to the God of Jacob. Take a psalm, and bring hither the timbrel: the pleasant psaltery with the harp. Blow up the trumpet on the new moon, on the noted day of your solemnity. For it is a commandment in Israel, and a judgment to the God of Jacob. He ordained it for a testimony in Joseph, when he came out of the land of Egypt: he heard a tongue which he knew not. He removed his back from the burdens: his hands had served in baskets. Thou calledst upon me in affliction, and I delivered thee: I heard thee in the secret place of tempest: I proved thee at the waters of contradiction. Hear, O my people, and I will testify to thee: O Israel, if thou wilt hearken to me, there shall be no new god in thee: neither shalt thou adore a strange god. For I am the LORD thy God, who brought thee out of the land of Egypt: open thy mouth wide, and I will fill it. But my people heard not my voice: and Israel hearkened not to me. So I let them go according to the desires of their heart: they shall walk in their own inventions. If my people had heard me: if Israel had walked in my ways: I should soon have humbled their enemies, and laid my hand on them that troubled them. The enemies of the LORD have lied to him: and their time shall be forever. And he fed them with the fat of wheat, and filled them with honey out of the rock.

81

Deus stetit

God hath stood in the congregation of gods: and being in the midst of them he judgeth gods. How long will you judge unjustly: and accept the persons of the wicked? Judge for the needy and fatherless: do justice to the humble and the poor. Rescue the poor; and deliver the needy out of the hand of the sinner. They have not known nor understood: they walk on in darkness: all the foundations of the earth shall be moved. I have said: You are gods and all of you the sons of the Most High. But you like men shall die: and shall fall like one of the princes. Arise, O God, judge thou the earth: for thou shalt inherit among all the nations.

82

Deus, quis similis

O God, who shall be like to thee? hold not thy peace, neither be thou still, O God. For lo, thy enemies have made a noise: and they that hate thee have lifted up the head. They have taken a malicious counsel against thy people, and have consulted against thy saints. They have said: Come and let us destroy them, so that they be not a nation: and let the name of Israel be remembered no more. For they have contrived with one consent: they have made a covenant together against thee, The tabernacles of the Edomites, and the Ismahelites: Moab, and the Agarens, Gebal, and Ammon and Amalec: the Philistines, with the inhabitants of Tyre. Yea, and the Assyrian also is joined with them: they are come to the aid of the sons of Lot. Do to them as thou didst to Madian and to Sisara: as to Jabin at the brook of Cisson. Who perished at Endor: and became as dung for the earth. Make their princes like Oreb, and Zeb, and Zebee, and Salmana. All their princes, who have said: Let us possess the sanctuary of God for an inheritance. O my God, make them like a wheel; and as stubble before the wind. As fire which burneth the wood: and as a flame burning mountains: So shalt thou pursue them with thy tempest: and shalt trouble them in thy wrath. Fill their faces with shame; and they shall seek thy name, O LORD. Let them be ashamed and troubled for ever and ever: and let them be confounded and perish. And let them know that the Lord is thy name: thou alone art the Most High over all the earth.

83

Quam dilecta

How lovely are thy tabernacles, O LORD of hosts! My soul longeth and fainteth for the courts of the LORD. My heart and my flesh have rejoiced in the living God. For the sparrow hath found herself a house, and the turtle a nest for herself where she may lay her young ones: Thy altars, O LORD of hosts, my king and my God. Blessed are they that dwell in thy house, O LORD: they shall praise thee for ever and ever. Blessed is the man whose help is from thee: in his heart he hath disposed to ascend by steps, In the vale of tears, in the place which he hath set. For the lawgiver shall give a blessing, they shall go from virtue to virtue: the God of gods shall be seen in Sion. O LORD God of hosts, hear my prayer: give ear, O God of Jacob. Behold, O God our protector: and look on the face of thy Christ. For better is one day in thy courts above thousands. I have chosen to be an abject in the house of my God, rather than to dwell in the tabernacles of sinners. For God loveth mercy and truth: the LORD will give grace and glory. He will not deprive of good things them that walk in innocence: O LORD of hosts, blessed is the man that trusteth in thee.

84

Benedixisti, Domine

LORD, thou hast blessed thy land: thou hast turned away the captivity of Jacob. Thou hast forgiven the iniquity of thy people: thou hast covered all their sins. Thou hast mitigated all thy anger: thou hast turned away from the wrath of thy indignation. Convert us, O God our saviour: and turn off thy anger from us. Wilt thou be angry with us forever: or wilt thou extend thy wrath from generation to generation? Thou wilt turn, O God, and bring us to life: and thy people shall rejoice in thee. Shew us, O LORD, thy mercy; and grant us thy salvation. I will hear what the LORD God will speak in me: for he will speak peace unto his people: And unto his saints: and unto them that are converted to the heart. Surely his salvation is near to them that fear him: that glory may dwell in our land. Mercy and truth have met each other: justice and peace have kissed. Truth is sprung out of the earth: and justice hath looked down from heaven. For the LORD will give goodness: and our earth shall yield her fruit. Justice shall walk before him: and shall set his steps in the way.

85

Inclina, Domine

Incline thy ear, O LORD, and hear me: for I am needy and poor. Preserve my soul, for I am holy: save thy servant, O my God, that trusteth in thee. Have mercy on me, O LORD, for I have cried to thee all the day. Give joy to the soul of thy servant, for to thee, O LORD, I have lifted up my soul. For thou, O LORD, art sweet and mild: and plenteous in mercy to all that call upon thee. Give ear, O LORD, to my prayer: and attend to the voice of my petition. I have called upon thee in the day of my trouble: because thou hast heard me. There is none among the gods like unto thee, O LORD: and there is none according to thy works. All the nations thou hast made shall come and adore before thee, O LORD: and they shall glorify thy name. For thou art great and dost wonderful things: thou art God alone. Conduct me, O LORD, in thy way, and I will walk in thy truth: let my heart rejoice that it may fear thy name. I will praise thee, O LORD my God: with my whole heart, and I will glorify thy name forever: For thy mercy is great towards me: and thou hast delivered my soul out of the lower hell. O God, the wicked are risen up against me, and the assembly of the mighty have sought my soul: and they have not set thee before their eyes. And thou, O LORD, art a God of compassion, and merciful, patient, and of much mercy, and true. O look upon me, and have mercy on me: give thy command to thy servant, and save the son of thy handmaid. Shew me a token for good: that they who hate me may see, and be confounded, because thou, O LORD, hast helped me and hast comforted me.

86

Fundamenta ejus

The foundations thereof are in the holy mountains: The LORD loveth the gates of Zion above all the tabernacles of Jacob. Glorious things are said of thee, O city of God. I will be mindful of Rahab and of Babylon knowing me. Behold the foreigners, and Tyre, and the people of the Ethiopians, these were there. Shall not Zion say: This man and that man is born in her? and the Highest himself hath founded her. The LORD shall tell in his writings of peoples and of princes, of them that have been in her. The dwelling in thee is as it were of all rejoicing.

87

Domine, Deus salutis

O LORD, the God of my salvation: I have cried in the day, and in the night before thee. Let my prayer come in before thee: incline thy ear to my petition. For my soul is filled with evils: and my life hath drawn nigh to hell. I am counted among them that go down to the pit: I am become as a man without help, Free among the dead. Like the slain sleeping in the sepulchres, whom thou rememberest no more: and they are cast off from thy hand. They have laid me in the lower pit: in the dark places, and in the shadow of death. Thy wrath is strong over me: and all thy waves thou hast brought in upon me. Thou hast put away my acquaintance far from me: they have set me an abomination to themselves. I was delivered up, and came not forth: My eyes languished through poverty. All the day I cried to thee, O LORD: I stretched out my hands to thee. Wilt thou shew wonders to the dead? or shall physicians raise to life, and give praise to thee? Shall any one in the sepulchre declare thy mercy: and thy truth in destruction? Shall thy wonders be known in the dark; and thy justice in the land of forgetfulness? But I, O LORD, have cried to thee: and in the morning my prayer shall prevent thee. LORD, why castest thou off my prayer: why turnest thou away thy face from me? I am poor, and in labours from my youth: and being exalted have been humbled and troubled. Thy wrath hath come upon me: and thy terrors have troubled me. They have come round about me like water all the day: they have compassed me about together. Friend and neighbour thou hast put far from me: and my acquaintance, because of misery.

88

Misericordias Domini

The mercies of the LORD I will sing forever. I will shew forth thy truth with my mouth to generation and generation. For thou hast said: Mercy shall be built up for ever in the heavens: thy truth shall be prepared in them. I have made a covenant with my elect: I have sworn to David my servant: Thy seed will I settle for ever. And I will build up thy throne unto generation and generation. The heavens shall confess thy wonders, O LORD: and thy truth in the church of the saints. For who in the clouds can be compared to the LORD: or who among the sons of God shall be like to God? God, who is glorified in the assembly of the saints: great and terrible above all them that are about him. O LORD God of hosts, who is like to thee? thou art mighty, O LORD, and thy truth is round about thee. Thou rulest the power of the sea: and appeasest the motion of the waves thereof. Thou hast humbled the proud one, as one that is slain: with the arm of thy strength thou hast scattered thy enemies. Thine are the heavens, and thine is the earth: the world and the fulness thereof thou hast founded: The north and the sea thou hast created. Thabor and Hermon shall rejoice in thy name: Thy arm is with might. Let thy hand be strengthened, and thy right hand exalted: Justice and judgment are the preparation of thy throne. Mercy and truth shall go before thy face: Blessed is the people that knoweth jubilation. They shall walk, O LORD, in the light of thy countenance: And in thy name they shall rejoice all the day, and in thy justice they shall be exalted. For thou art the glory of their strength: and in thy good pleasure shall our horn be exalted. For our protection is of the LORD, and of our king the holy one of Israel. Then thou spokest in a vision to thy saints, and saidst: I have laid help upon one that is mighty, and have exalted one chosen out of my people. I have found David my servant: with my holy oil I have anointed him. For my hand shall help him: and my arm shall strengthen him. The enemy shall have no advantage over him: nor the son of iniquity have power to hurt him. And I will cut down his enemies before his face; and them that hate him I will put to flight. And my truth and my mercy shall be with him: and in my name shall his horn be exalted. And I will set his hand in the sea; and his right hand in the rivers. He shall cry out to me: Thou art my father: my God, and the support of my salvation. And I will make him my firstborn, high above the kings of the earth. I will keep my mercy for him forever: and my covenant faithful to him. And I will make his seed to endure forevermore: and his throne as the days of heaven. And if his children forsake my law, and walk not in my judgments: If they profane my justices: and keep not my commandments: I will visit their iniquities with a rod: and their sins with stripes. But my mercy I will not take away from him: nor will I suffer my truth to fail. Neither will I profane my covenant: and the words that proceed from my mouth I will not make void. Once have I sworn by my holiness: I will not lie unto David: His seed shall endure forever. And his throne as the sun before me: and as the moon perfect for ever, and a faithful witness in heaven. But thou hast rejected and despised: thou hast been angry with thy anointed. Thou hast overthrown the covenant of thy servant: thou hast profaned his sanctuary on the earth. Thou hast broken down all his hedges: thou hast made his strength fear. All that pass by the way have robbed him: he is become a reproach to his neighbours. Thou hast set up the right hand of them that oppress him: thou hast made all his enemies to rejoice. Thou hast turned away the help of his sword; and hast not assisted him in battle. Thou hast made his purification to cease: and thou hast cast his throne down to the ground. Thou hast shortened the days of his time: thou hast covered him with confusion. How long, O LORD, turnest thou away unto the end? shall thy anger burn like fire? Remember what my substance is for hast thou made all the children of men in vain? Who is the man that shall live, and not see death: that shall deliver his soul from the hand of hell? LORD, where are thy ancient mercies, according to what thou didst swear to David in thy truth? Be mindful, O LORD, of the reproach of thy servants (which I have held in my bosom) of many nations: Wherewith thy enemies have reproached, O LORD; wherewith they have reproached the change of thy anointed. Blessed be the LORD for evermore. So be it. So be it.

90

Qui habitat

He that dwelleth in the aid of the Most High, shall abide under the protection of the God of Jacob. He shall say to the LORD: Thou art my protector, and my refuge: my God, in him will I trust. For he hath delivered me from the snare of the hunters: and from the sharp word. He will overshadow thee with his shoulders: and under his wings thou shalt trust. His truth shall compass thee with a shield: thou shalt not be afraid of the terror of the night. Of the arrow that flieth in the day, of the business that walketh about in the dark: of invasion, or of the noonday devil. A thousand shall fall at thy side, and ten thousand at thy right hand: but it shall not come nigh thee. But thou shalt consider with thy eyes: and shalt see the reward of the wicked. Because thou, O LORD, art my hope: thou hast made the Most High thy refuge. There shall no evil come to thee: nor shall the scourge come near thy dwelling. For he hath given his angels charge over thee; to keep thee in all thy ways. In their hands they shall bear thee up: lest thou dash thy foot against a stone. Thou shalt walk upon the asp and the basilisk: and thou shalt trample under foot the lion and the dragon. Because he hoped in me I will deliver him: I will protect him because he hath known my name. He shall cry to me, and I will hear him: I am with him in tribulation, I will deliver him, and I will glorify him. I will fill him with length of days; and I will shew him my salvation.

91

Bonum est confiteri

It is good to give praise to the LORD: and to sing to thy name, O Most High. To shew forth thy mercy in the morning, and thy truth in the night: Upon an instrument of ten strings, upon the psaltery: with a canticle upon the harp. For thou hast given me, O LORD, a delight in thy doings: and in the works of thy hands I shall rejoice. O LORD, how great are thy works! thy thoughts are exceeding deep. The senseless man shall not know: nor will the fool understand these things. When the wicked shall spring up as grass: and all the workers of iniquity shall appear: That they may perish forever and ever: But thou, O LORD, art most high forevermore. For behold thy enemies, O LORD, for behold thy enemies shall perish: and all the workers of iniquity shall be scattered. But my horn shall be exalted like that of the unicorn: and my old age in plentiful mercy. My eye also hath looked down upon my enemies: and my ear shall hear of the downfall of the malignant that rise up against me. The just shall flourish like the palm tree: he shall grow up like the cedar of Libanus. They that are planted in the house of the LORD shall flourish in the courts of the house of our God. They shall still increase in a fruitful old age: and shall be well treated, that they may shew, that the LORD our God is righteous, and there is no iniquity in him.

92

Dominus regnavit

The LORD hath reigned, he is clothed with beauty: the LORD is clothed with strength, and hath girded himself. For he hath established the world which shall not be moved. Thy throne is prepared from of old: thou art from everlasting. The floods have lifted up, O LORD: the floods have lifted up their voice. The floods have lifted up their waves, With the noise of many waters. Wonderful are the surges of the sea: wonderful is the LORD on high. Thy testimonies are become exceedingly credible: holiness becometh thy house, O LORD, unto length of days.

Session Eight

93

Deus ultionum

The LORD is the God to whom revenge belongeth: the God of revenge hath acted freely. Lift up thyself, thou that judgest the earth: render a reward to the proud. How long shall sinners, O LORD: how long shall sinners glory? Shall they utter, and speak iniquity: shall all speak who work injustice? Thy people, O LORD, they have brought low: and they have afflicted thy inheritance. They have slain the widow and the stranger: and they have murdered the fatherless. And they have said: The LORD shall not see: neither shall the God of Jacob understand. Understand, ye senseless among the people: and, you fools, be wise at last. He that planted the ear, shall he not hear? or he that formed the eye, doth he not consider? He that chastiseth nations, shall he not rebuke: he that teacheth man knowledge? The LORD knoweth the thoughts of men, that they are vain. Blessed is the man whom thou shalt instruct, O LORD: and shalt teach him out of thy law. That thou mayst give him rest from the evil days: till a pit be dug for the wicked. For the LORD will not cast off his people: neither will he forsake his own inheritance. Until justice be turned into judgment: and they that are near it are all the upright in heart. Who shall rise up for me against the evildoers? or who shall stand with me against the workers of iniquity? Unless the LORD had been my helper, my soul had almost dwelt in hell. If I said: My foot is moved: thy mercy, O LORD, assisted me. According to the multitude of my sorrows in my heart, thy comforts have given joy to my soul. Doth the seat of iniquity stick to thee, who framest labour in commandment? They will hunt after the soul of the just, and will condemn innocent blood. But the LORD is my refuge: and my God the help of my hope. And he will render them their iniquity: and in their malice he will destroy them: the LORD our God will destroy them.

94

Venite exultemus

Come let us praise the LORD with joy: let us joyfully sing to God our saviour. Let us come before his presence with thanksgiving; and make a joyful noise to him with psalms. For the LORD is a great God, and a great King above all gods. For in his hand are all the ends of the earth: and the heights of the mountains are his. For the sea is his, and he made it: and his hands formed the dry land. Come let us adore and fall down: and weep before the LORD that made us. For he is the LORD our God: and we are the people of his pasture and the sheep of his hand. Today if you shall hear his voice, harden not your hearts: As in the provocation, according to the day of temptation in the wilderness: where your fathers tempted me, they proved me, and saw my works. Forty years long was I offended with that generation, and I said: These always err in heart. And these men have not known my ways: so I swore in my wrath that they shall not enter into my rest.

95

Cantate Domino

Sing ye to the LORD a new canticle: sing to the LORD, all the earth. Sing ye to the LORD and bless his name: shew forth his salvation from day to day. Declare his glory among the Gentiles: his wonders among all people. For the LORD is great, and exceedingly to be praised: he is to be feared above all gods. For all the gods of the Gentiles are devils: but the LORD made the heavens. Praise and beauty are before him: holiness and majesty in his sanctuary. Bring ye to the LORD, O ye kindreds of the Gentiles, bring ye to the LORD glory and honour: Bring to the LORD glory unto his name. Bring up sacrifices, and come into his courts: Adore ye the LORD in his holy court. Let all the earth be moved at his presence. Say ye among the Gentiles, the LORD hath reigned. For he hath corrected the world, which shall not be moved: he will judge the people with justice. Let the heavens rejoice, and let the earth be glad, let the sea be moved, and the fulness thereof: The fields and all things that are in them shall be joyful. Then shall all the trees of the woods rejoice before the face of the LORD, because he cometh: because he cometh to judge the earth. He shall judge the world with justice, and the people with his truth.

96

Dominus regnavit

For the same David, when his land was restored again to him. The LORD hath reigned, let the earth rejoice: let many islands be glad. Clouds and darkness are round about him: justice and judgment are the establishment of his throne. A fire shall go before him, and shall burn his enemies round about. His lightnings have shone forth to the world: the earth saw and trembled. The mountains melted like wax, at the presence of the LORD: at the presence of the LORD of all the earth. The heavens declared his justice: and all people saw his glory. Let them be all confounded that adore graven things, and that glory in their idols. Adore him, all you his angels: Zion heard, and was glad. And the daughters of Judah rejoiced, because of thy judgments, O LORD. For thou art the Most High LORD over all the earth: thou art exalted exceedingly above all gods. You that love the LORD, hate evil: the LORD preserveth the souls of his saints, he will deliver them out of the hand of the sinner. Light is risen to the just, and joy to the right of heart. Rejoice, ye just, in the LORD: and give praise to the remembrance of his holiness.

97

Cantate Domino

Sing ye to the LORD a new canticle: because he hath done wonderful things. His right hand hath wrought for him salvation, and his arm is holy. The LORD hath made known his salvation: he hath revealed his justice in the sight of the Gentiles. He hath remembered his mercy and his truth toward the house of Israel. All the ends of the earth have seen the salvation of our God. Sing joyfully to God, all the earth; make melody, rejoice and sing. Sing praise to the LORD on the harp, on the harp, and with the voice of a psalm: With long trumpets, and sound of cornet. Make a joyful noise before the LORD our king: Let the sea be moved and the fulness thereof: the world and they that dwell therein. The rivers shall clap their hands, the mountains shall rejoice together At the presence of the LORD: because he cometh to judge the earth. He shall judge the world with justice, and the people with equity.

98

Dominus regnavit

The LORD hath reigned, let the people be angry: he that sitteth on the cherubims: let the earth be moved. The LORD is great in Zion, and high above all people. Let them give praise to thy great name: for it is terrible and holy: And the king's honour loveth judgment. Thou hast prepared directions: thou hast done judgment and justice in Jacob. Exalt ye the LORD our God, and adore his footstool, for it is holy. Moses and Aaron among his priests: and Samuel among them that call upon his name. They called upon the LORD, and he heard them: He spoke to them in the pillar of the cloud. They kept his testimonies, and the commandment which he gave them. Thou didst hear them, O LORD our God: thou wast a merciful God to them, and taking vengeance on all their inventions. Exalt ye the Lord our God, and adore at his holy mountain: for the LORD our God is holy.

99

Jubilate Deo

Sing joyfully to God, all the earth: serve ye the LORD with gladness. Come in before his presence with exceeding great joy. Know ye that the LORD he is God: he made us, and not we ourselves. We are his people and the sheep of his pasture. Go ye into his gates with praise, into his courts with hymns: and give glory to him. Praise ye his name: For the LORD is sweet, his mercy endureth forever, and his truth to generation and generation.

100

Misericordiam et judicium

Mercy and judgment I will sing to thee, O LORD: I will sing, And I will understand in the unspotted way, when thou shalt come to me. I walked in the innocence of my heart, in the midst of my house. I did not set before my eyes any unjust thing: I hated the workers of iniquities. The perverse heart did not cleave to me: and the malignant, that turned aside from me, I would not know. The man that in private detracted his neighbour, him did I persecute. With him that had a proud eye, and an unsatiable heart, I would not eat. My eyes were upon the faithful of the earth, to sit with me: the man that walked in the perfect way, he served me. He that worketh pride shall not dwell in the midst of my house: he that speaketh unjust things did not prosper before my eyes. In the morning I put to death all the wicked of the land: that I might cut off all the workers of iniquity from the city of the LORD.

101

Domine, exaudi

Hear, O LORD, my prayer: and let my cry come to thee. Turn not away thy face from me: in the day when I am in trouble, incline thy ear to me. In what day soever I shall call upon thee, hear me speedily. For my days are vanished like smoke: and my bones are grown dry like fuel for the fire. I am smitten as grass, and my heart is withered: because I forgot to eat my bread. Through the voice of my groaning, my bone hath cleaved to my flesh. I am become like to a pelican of the wilderness: I am like a night raven in the house. I have watched, and am become as a sparrow all alone on the house-top. All the day long my enemies reproached me: and they that praised me did swear against me. For I did eat ashes like bread, and mingled my drink with weeping. Because of thy anger and indignation: for having lifted me up thou hast thrown me down. My days have declined like a shadow, and I am withered like grass. But thou, O LORD, endurest forever: and thy memorial to all generations. Thou shalt arise and have mercy on Zion: for it is time to have mercy on it, for the time is come. For the stones thereof have pleased thy servants: and they shall have pity on the earth thereof. And the Gentiles shall fear thy name, O LORD, and all the kings of the earth thy glory. For the Lord hath built up Zion: and he shall be seen in his glory. He hath had regard to the prayer of the humble: and he hath not despised their petition. Let these things be written unto another generation: and the people that shall be created shall praise the LORD: Because he hath looked forth from his high sanctuary: from heaven the LORD hath looked upon the earth. That he might hear the groans of them that are in fetters: that he might release the children of the slain: That they may declare the name of the LORD in Zion: and his praise in Jerusalem; When the people assemble together, and kings, to serve the LORD. He answered him in the way of his strength: Declare unto me the fewness of my days. Call me not away in the midst of my days: thy years are unto generation and generation. In the beginning, O LORD, thou foundedst the earth: and the heavens are the works of thy hands. They shall perish but thou remainest: and all of them shall grow old like a garment: And as a vesture thou shalt change them, and they shall be changed. But thou art always the selfsame, and thy years shall not fail. The children of thy servants shall continue: and their seed shall be directed forever.

102

Benedic, anima

Bless the LORD, O my soul: and let all that is within me bless his holy name. Bless the LORD, O my soul, and never forget all he hath done for thee. Who forgiveth all thy iniquities: who healeth all thy diseases. Who redeemeth thy life from destruction: who crowneth thee with mercy and compassion. Who satisfieth thy desire with good things: thy youth shall be renewed like the eagle's. The LORD doth mercies, and judgment for all that suffer wrong. He hath made his ways known to Moses: his wills to the children of Israel. The LORD is compassionate and merciful: longsuffering and plenteous in mercy. He will not always be angry: nor will he threaten forever. He hath not dealt with us according to our sins: nor rewarded us according to our iniquities. For according to the height of the heaven above the earth: he hath strengthened his mercy towards them that fear him. As far as the east is from the west, so far hath he removed our iniquities from us. As a father hath compassion on his children, so hath the LORD compassion on them that fear him: For he knoweth our frame. He remembereth that we are dust: Man's days are as grass, as the flower of the field so shall he flourish. For the spirit shall pass in him, and he shall not be: and he shall know his place no more. But the mercy of the LORD is from eternity and unto eternity upon them that fear him: And his justice unto children's children, to such as keep his covenant, and are mindful of his commandments to do them. The LORD hath prepared his throne in heaven: and his kingdom shall rule over all. Bless the Lord, all ye his angels: you that are mighty in strength, and execute his word, hearkening to the voice of his orders. Bless the LORD, all ye his hosts: you ministers of his that do his will. Bless the LORD, all his works: in every place of his dominion, O my soul, bless thou the LORD.

104

Confitemini Domino

Alleluia. Give glory to the LORD, and call upon his name: declare his deeds among the Gentiles. Sing to him, yea sing praises to him: relate all his wondrous works. Glory ye in his holy name: let the heart of them rejoice that seek the LORD. Seek ye the LORD, and be strengthened: seek his face evermore. Remember his marvellous works which he hath done; his wonders, and the judgments of his mouth. O ye seed of Abraham his servant; ye sons of Jacob his chosen. He is the LORD our God: his judgments are in all the earth. He hath remembered his covenant forever: the word which he commanded to a thousand generations. Which he made to Abraham; and his oath to Isaac: And he appointed the same to Jacob for a law, and to Israel for an everlasting testament: Saying: To thee will I give the land of Chanaan, the lot of your inheritance. When they were but a small number: yea very few, and sojourners therein: And they passed from nation to nation, and from one kingdom to another people. He suffered no man to hurt them: and he reproved kings for their sakes. Touch ye not my anointed: and do no evil to my prophets. And he called a famine upon the land: and he broke in pieces all the support of bread. He sent a man before them: Joseph, who was sold for a slave. They humbled his feet in fetters: the iron pierced his soul, until his word came. The word of the LORD inflamed him. The king sent, and he released him: the ruler of the people, and he set him at liberty. He made him master of his house, and ruler of all his possession. That he might instruct his princes as himself, and teach his ancients wisdom. And Israel went into Egypt: and Jacob was a sojourner in the land of Cham. And he increased his people exceedingly: and strengthened them over their enemies, He turned their heart to hate his people: and to deal deceitfully with his servants. He sent Moses his servant: Aaron the man whom he had chosen. He gave them power to shew his signs, and his wonders in the land of Cham. He sent darkness, and made it obscure: and grieved not his words. He turned their waters into blood, and destroyed their fish. Their land brought forth frogs, in the inner chambers of their kings. He spoke, and there came divers sorts of flies and sciniphs in all their coasts. He gave them hail for rain, a burning fire in the land. And he destroyed their vineyards and their fig trees: and he broke in pieces the trees of their coasts. He spoke, and the locust came, and the bruchus, of which there was no number. And they devoured all the grass in their land, and consumed all the fruit of their ground. And he slew all the firstborn in their land: the firstfruits of all their labour. And he brought them out with silver and gold: and there was not among their tribes one that was feeble. Egypt was glad when they departed: for the fear of them lay upon them. He spread a cloud for their protection, and fire to give them light in the night. They asked, and the quail came: and he filled them with the bread of heaven. He opened the rock, and waters flowed: rivers ran down in the dry land. Because he remembered his holy word, which he had spoken to his servant Abraham. And he brought forth his people with joy, and his chosen with gladness. And he gave them the lands of the Gentiles: and they possessed the labours of the people: That they might observe his justifications, and seek after his law.

105

Confitemini Domino

Alleluia. Give glory to the LORD, for he is good: for his mercy endureth forever. Who shall declare the powers of the LORD? who shall set forth all his praises? Blessed are they that keep judgment and do justice at all times. Remember us, O LORD, in the favour of thy people: visit us with thy salvation. That we may see the good of thy chosen, that we may rejoice in the joy of thy nation: that thou mayst be praised with thy inheritance. We have sinned with our fathers: we have acted unjustly, we have wrought iniquity. Our fathers understood not thy wonders in Egypt: they remembered not the multitude of thy mercies: And they provoked to wrath going up to the sea, even the Red Sea. And he saved them for his own name's sake: that he might make his power known. And he rebuked the Red Sea, and it was dried up: and he led them through the depths, as in a wilderness. And he saved them from the hand of them that hated them: and he redeemed them from the hand of the enemy. And the water covered them that afflicted them: there was not one of them left. And they believed his words: and they sang his praises. They had quickly done, they forgot his works: and they waited not for his counsels. And they coveted their desire in the desert: and they tempted God in the place without water. And he gave them their request: and sent fulness into their souls. And they provoked Moses in the camp, Aaron the holy one of the LORD. The earth opened and swallowed up Dathan: and covered the congregation of Abiron. And a fire was kindled in their congregation: the flame burned the wicked. They made also a calf in Horeb: and they adored the graven thing. And they changed their glory into the likeness of a calf that eateth grass. They forgot God, who saved them, who had done great things in Egypt, wondrous works in the land of Cham: terrible things in the Red Sea. And he said that he would destroy them: had not Moses his chosen stood before him in the breach: To turn away his wrath, lest he should destroy them. And they set at nought the desirable land. They believed not his word, and they murmured in their tents: they hearkened not to the voice of the LORD. And he lifted up his hand over them: to overthrow them in the desert; And to cast down their seed among the nations, and to scatter them in the countries. They also were initiated to Beelphegor: and ate the sacrifices of the dead. And they provoked him with their inventions: and destruction was multiplied among them. Then Phinees stood up, and pacified him: and the slaughter ceased. And it was reputed to him unto justice, to generation and generation forevermore. They provoked him also at the waters of contradiction: and Moses was afflicted for their sakes: Because they exasperated his spirit. And he distinguished with his lips. They did not destroy the nations of which the LORD spoke unto them. And they were mingled among the heathens, and learned their works: And served their idols, and it became a stumbling block to them. And they sacrificed their sons, and their daughters to devils. And they shed innocent blood: the blood of their sons and of their daughters which they sacrificed to the idols of Chanaan. And the land was polluted with blood, and was defiled with their works: and they went aside after their own inventions. And the LORD was exceedingly angry with his people: and he abhorred his inheritance. And he delivered them into the hands of the nations: and they that hated them had dominion over them. And their enemies afflicted them: and they were humbled under their hands: Many times did he deliver them. But they provoked him with their counsel: and they were brought low by their iniquities. And he saw when they were in tribulation: and he heard their prayer. And he was mindful of his covenant: and repented according to the multitude of his mercies. And he gave them unto mercies, in the sight of all those that had made them captives. Save us, O LORD, our God: and gather us from among nations: That we may give thanks to thy holy name, and may glory in thy praise. Blessed be the LORD the God of Israel, from everlasting to everlasting: and let all the people say: So be it, so be it.

Session Nine

106

Confitemini Domino

Give glory to the LORD, for he is good: for his mercy endureth forever. Let them say so that have been redeemed by the LORD, whom he hath redeemed from the hand of the enemy: and gathered out of the countries. From the rising and the setting of the sun, from the north and from the sea. They wandered in a wilderness, in a place without water: they found not the way of a city for their habitation. They were hungry and thirsty: their soul fainted in them. And they cried to the LORD in their tribulation: and he delivered them out of their distresses. And he led them into the right way: that they might go to a city of habitation. Let the mercies of the LORD give glory to him: and his wonderful works to the children of men. For he hath satisfied the empty soul, and hath filled the hungry soul with good things. Such as sat in darkness and in the shadow of death: bound in want and in iron. Because they had exasperated the words of God: and provoked the counsel of the Most High: And their heart was humbled with labours: they were weakened, and there was none to help them. Then they cried to the LORD in their affliction: and he delivered them out of their distresses. And he brought them out of darkness, and the shadow of death; and broke their bonds in sunder. Let the mercies of the LORD give glory to him, and his wonderful works to the children of men. Because he hath broken gates of brass, and burst the iron bars. He took them out of the way of their iniquity: for they were brought low for their injustices. Their soul abhorred all manner of meat: and they drew nigh even to the gates of death. And they cried to the LORD in their affliction: and he delivered them out of their distresses. He sent his word, and healed them: and delivered them from their destructions. Let the mercies of the LORD give glory to him: and his wonderful works to the children of men. And let them sacrifice the sacrifice of praise: and declare his works with joy. They that go down to the sea in ships, doing business in the great waters: These have seen the works of the LORD, and his wonders in the deep. He said the word, and there arose a storm of wind: and the waves thereof were lifted up. They mount up to the heavens, and they go down to the depths: their soul pined away with evils. They were troubled, and reeled like a drunken man; and all their wisdom was swallowed up. And they cried to the LORD in their affliction:

and he brought them out of their distresses. And he turned the storm into a breeze: and its waves were still. And they rejoiced because they were still: and he brought them to the haven which they wished for. Let the mercies of the LORD give glory to him, and his wonderful works to the children of men. And let them exalt him in the church of the people: and praise him in the chair of the ancients. He hath turned rivers into a wilderness: and the sources of water into dry ground: A fruitful land into barrenness, for the wickedness of them that dwell therein. He hath turned a wilderness into pools of water, and a dry land into water springs. And hath placed there the hungry; and they made a city for their habitation. And they sowed fields, and planted vineyards: and they yielded fruit of birth. And he blessed them, and they were multiplied exceedingly: and their cattle he suffered not to decrease. Then they were brought to be few: and they were afflicted through the trouble of evils and sorrow. Contempt was poured forth upon their princes: and he caused them to wander where there was no passing, and out of the way. And he helped the poor out of poverty: and made him families like a flock of sheep. The just shall see, and shall rejoice, and all iniquity shall stop their mouth. Who is wise, and will keep these things: and will understand the mercies of the LORD?

107

Paratum cor meum

My heart is ready, O God, my heart is ready: I will sing, and will give praise, with my glory. Arise, my glory; arise, psaltery and harp: I will arise in the morning early. I will praise thee, O LORD, among the people: and I will sing unto thee among the populations. For thy mercy is great above the heavens: and thy truth even unto the clouds. Be thou exalted, O God, above the heavens, and thy glory over all the earth: That thy beloved may be delivered. Save with thy right hand and hear me. God hath spoken in his holiness. I will rejoice, and I will divide Sichem and I will mete out the vale of tabernacles. Galaad is mine, and Manasses is mine and Ephraim the protection of my head. Juda is my king: Moab the pot of my hope. Over Edom I will stretch out my shoe: the aliens are become my friends. Who will bring me into the strong city? who will lead me into Edom? Wilt not thou, O God, who hast cast us off? and wilt not thou, O God, go forth with our armies?

O grant us help from trouble: for vain is the help of man. Through God we shall do mightily: and he will bring our enemies to nothing.

108

Deus, laudem meam

O God, be not thou silent in my praise: for the mouth of the wicked and the mouth of the deceitful man is opened against me. They have spoken against me with deceitful tongues; and they have compassed me about with words of hatred; and have fought against me without cause. Instead of making me a return of love, they detracted me: but I gave myself to prayer. And they repaid me evil for good: and hatred for my love. Set thou the sinner over him: and may the devil stand at his right hand. When he is judged, may he go out condemned; and may his prayer be turned to sin. May his days be few: and his bishopric let another take. May his children be fatherless, and his wife a widow. Let his children be carried about vagabonds and beg; and let them be cast out of their dwellings. May the usurer search all his substance: and let strangers plunder his labours. May there be none to help him: nor none to pity his fatherless offspring. May his posterity be cut off; in one generation may his name be blotted out. May the iniquity of his fathers be remembered in the sight of the LORD: and let not the sin of his mother be blotted out. May they be before the LORD continually, and let the memory of them perish from the earth: because he remembered not to shew mercy, But persecuted the poor man and the beggar; and the broken in heart, to put him to death. And he loved cursing, and it shall come unto him: and he would not have blessing, and it shall be far from him. And he put on cursing, like a garment: and it went in like water into his entrails, and like oil in his bones. May it be unto him like a garment which covereth him; and like a girdle with which he is girded continually. This is the work of them who detract me before the LORD; and who speak evils against my soul. But thou, O LORD, do with me for thy name's sake: because thy mercy is sweet. Do thou deliver me, for I am poor and needy, and my heart is troubled within me. I am taken away like the shadow when it declineth: and I am shaken off as locusts. My knees are weakened through fasting: and my flesh is changed for oil. And I am become a reproach to them: they saw me and they shaked their heads, Help me, O LORD my God; save me according to thy mercy. And let them know that this is thy hand: and that thou, O LORD, hast done it. They will curse and thou will bless: let them that rise up against me be confounded: but thy servant shall rejoice. Let them that detract me be clothed with shame: and let them be covered with their confusion as with a double cloak. I will give great thanks to the LORD with my mouth: and in the midst of many I will praise him. Because he hath stood at the right hand of the poor, to save my soul from persecutors.

109

Dixit Dominus

The LORD said to my LORD: Sit thou at my right hand: Until I make thy enemies thy footstool. The LORD will send forth the sceptre of thy power out of Sion: rule thou in the midst of thy enemies. With thee is the principality in the day of thy strength: in the brightness of the saints: from the womb before the day star I begot thee. The LORD hath sworn, and he will not repent: Thou art a priest forever according to the order of Melchisedech. The LORD at thy right hand hath broken kings in the day of his wrath. He shall judge among nations, he shall fill ruins: he shall crush the heads in the land of the many. He shall drink of the torrent in the way: therefore shall he lift up the head.

110

Confitebor tibi, Domine

I will praise thee, O LORD, with my whole heart; in the council of the just: and in the congregation. Great are the works of the LORD: sought out according to all his wills. His work is praise and magnificence: and his justice continueth forever and ever. He hath made a remembrance of his wonderful works, being a merciful and gracious LORD: He hath given food to them that fear him. He will be mindful forever of his covenant: He will shew forth to his people the power of his works. That he may give them the inheritance of the Gentiles: the works of his hands are truth and judgment. All his commandments are faithful: confirmed for ever and ever, made in truth and equity. He hath sent redemption to his people: he hath commanded his covenant forever. Holy and terrible is his name: The fear of the LORD is the beginning of wisdom. A good understanding to all that do it: his praise continueth forever and ever.

111

Beatus vir

Blessed is the man that feareth the LORD: he shall delight exceedingly in his commandments. His seed shall be mighty upon earth: the generation of the righteous shall be blessed. Glory and wealth shall be in his house: and his justice remaineth forever and ever. To the righteous a light is risen up in darkness: he is merciful, and compassionate and just. Acceptable is the man that sheweth mercy and lendeth: he shall order his words with judgment: Because he shall not be moved forever. The just shall be in everlasting remembrance: he shall not fear the evil hearing. His heart is ready to hope in the LORD: His heart is strengthened, he shall not be moved until he look over his enemies. He hath distributed, he hath given to the poor: his justice remaineth for ever and ever: his horn shall be exalted in glory. The wicked shall see, and shall be angry, he shall gnash with his teeth and pine away: the desire of the wicked shall perish.

113

In exitu Israel

When Israel went out of Egypt, the house of Jacob from a barbarous people: Judea was made his sanctuary, Israel his dominion. The sea saw and fled: Jordan was turned back. The mountains skipped like rams, and the hills like the lambs of the flock. What ailed thee, O thou sea, that thou didst flee: and thou, O Jordan, that thou wast turned back? Ye mountains, that ye skipped like rams, and ye hills, like lambs of the flock? At the presence of the LORD the earth was moved, at the presence of the God of Jacob: Who turned the rock into pools of water, and the stony hill into fountains of waters. Not to us, O LORD, not to us; but to thy name give glory. For thy mercy, and for thy truth's sake: lest the gentiles should say: Where is their God? But our God is in heaven: he hath done all things whatsoever he would. The idols of the gentiles are silver and gold, the works of the hands of men. They have mouths and speak not: they have eyes and see not. They have ears and hear not: they have noses and smell not. They have hands and feel not: they have feet and walk not: neither shall they cry out through their throat. Let them that make them become like unto them: and all such as trust in them. The house of Israel hath hoped in the LORD: he is their helper and their protector. The house of Aaron hath hoped in the LORD: he is their helper and their protector. They that fear the Lord hath hoped in the LORD: he is their helper and their protector. The LORD hath been mindful of us, and hath blessed us. He hath blessed the house of Israel: he hath blessed the house of Aaron. He hath blessed all that fear the LORD, both little and great. May the LORD add blessings upon you: upon you, and upon your children. Blessed be you of the LORD, who made heaven and earth. The heaven of heaven is the LORD's: but the earth he has given to the children of men. The dead shall not praise thee, O LORD: nor any of them that go down to hell. But we that live bless the Lord: from this time now and forever.

116

Laudate Dominum

O praise the LORD, all ye nations: praise him, all ye people. For his mercy is confirmed upon us: and the truth of the LORD remaineth forever.

117

Confitemini Domino

Give praise to the LORD, for he is good: for his mercy endureth forever. Let Israel now say that he is good: that his mercy endureth forever. Let the house of Aaron now say, that his mercy endureth forever. Let them that fear the LORD now say, that his mercy endureth forever. In my trouble I called upon the LORD: and the LORD heard me, and enlarged me. The LORD is my helper, I will not fear what man can do unto me. The LORD is my helper: and I will look over my enemies. It is good to confide in the LORD, rather than to have confidence in man. It is good to trust in the LORD, rather than to trust in princes. All nations compassed me about; and in the name of the LORD I have been revenged on them. Surrounding me they compassed me about: and in the name of the LORD I have been revenged on them. They surrounded me like bees, and they burned like fire among thorns: and in the name of the LORD I was revenged on them. Being pushed I was overturned that I might fall: but the LORD supported me. The LORD is my strength and my praise: and he is become my salvation. The voice of rejoicing and of salvation is in the tabernacles of the just. The right hand of the LORD hath wrought strength: the right hand of the Lord hath exulted me: the right hand of the LORD hath wrought strength. I shall not die, but live: and shall declare the works of the LORD. The LORD chastising hath chastised me: but he hath not delivered me over to death. Open ye to me the gates of justice: I will go into them, and give praise to the LORD. This is the gate of the LORD, the just shall enter into it. I will give glory to thee because thou hast heard me: and art become my salvation. The stone which the builders rejected; the same is become the head of the corner. This is the LORD's doing: and it is wonderful in our eyes. This is the day which the LORD hath made: let us be glad and rejoice therein. O LORD, save me: O LORD, give good success. Blessed be he that cometh in the name LORD. We have blessed you out of the house of the LORD. The LORD is God, and he hath shone upon us. Appoint a solemn day, with shady boughs, even to the horn of the altar. Thou art my God, and I will praise thee: thou art my God, and I will exalt thee. I will praise thee, because thou hast heard me, and art become my salvation. O praise ye the LORD, for he is good: for his mercy endureth forever.

118

Beati immaculati

ALEPH. Blessed are the undefiled in the way, who walk in the law of the LORD. Blessed are they who search his testimonies: that seek him with their whole heart. For they that work iniquity, have not walked in his ways. Thou hast commanded thy commandments to be kept most diligently. O! that my ways may be directed to keep thy justifications. Then shall I not be confounded, when I shall look into all thy commandments. I will praise thee with uprightness of heart, when I shall have learned the judgments of thy justice. I will keep thy justifications: O! do not thou utterly forsake me.

BETH. By what doth a young man correct his way? by observing thy words. With my whole heart have I sought after thee: let me not stray from thy commandments. Thy words have I hidden in my heart, that I may not sin against thee. Blessed art thou, O LORD: teach me thy justifications. With my lips I have pronounced all the judgments of thy mouth. I have been delighted in the way of thy testimonies, as in all riches. I will meditate on thy commandments: and I will consider thy ways. I will think of thy justifications: I will not forget thy words.

GIMEL. Give bountifully to thy servant, enliven me: and I shall keep thy words. Open thou my eyes: and I will consider the wondrous things of thy law. I am a sojourner on the earth: hide not thy commandments from me. My soul hath coveted to long for thy justifications, at all times. Thou hast rebuked the proud: they are cursed who decline from thy commandments. Remove from me reproach and contempt: because I have sought after thy testimonies. For princes sat, and spoke against me: but thy servant was employed in thy justifications. For thy testimonies are my meditation: and thy justifications my counsel.

DALETH. My soul hath cleaved to the pavement: quicken thou me according to thy word. I have declared my ways, and thou hast heard me: teach me thy justifications. Make me to understand the way of thy justifications: and I shall be exercised in thy wondrous works. My soul hath slumbered through heaviness: strengthen thou me in thy words. Remove from me the way of iniquity: and out of thy law have mercy on me. I have chosen the way of truth: thy judgments I have not forgotten. I have stuck to thy testimonies, O LORD: put me not to shame. I have run the way of thy commandments, when thou didst enlarge my heart.

HE. Set before me for a law the way of thy justifications, O LORD: and I will always seek after it. Give me understanding, and I will search thy law; and I will keep it with my whole heart. Lead me into the path of thy commandments; for this same I have desired. Incline my heart into thy testimonies and not to covetousness. Turn away my eyes that they may not behold vanity: quicken me in thy way. Establish thy word to thy servant, in thy fear. Turn away my reproach, which I have apprehended: for thy judgments are delightful. Behold I have longed after thy precepts: quicken me in thy justice.

VAU. Let thy mercy also come upon me, O LORD: thy salvation according to thy word. So shall I answer them that reproach me in anything; that I have trusted in thy words. And take not thou the word of truth utterly out of my mouth: for in thy words have I hoped exceedingly. So shall I always keep thy law, forever and ever. And I walked at large: because I have sought after thy commandments. And I spoke of thy testimonies before kings: and I was not ashamed. I meditated also on thy commandments, which I loved. And I lifted up my hands to thy commandments, which I loved: and I was exercised in thy justifications.

ZAIN. Be thou mindful of thy word to thy servant, in which thou hast given me hope. This hath comforted me in my humiliation: because thy word hath enlivened me. The proud did iniquitously altogether: but I declined not from thy law. I remembered, O LORD, thy judgments of old: and I was comforted. A fainting hath taken hold of me, because of the wicked that forsake thy law. Thy justifications were the subject of my song, in the place of my pilgrimage. In the night I have remembered thy name, O LORD: and have kept thy law. This happened to me: because I sought after thy justifications.

HETH. O LORD, my portion, I have said, I would keep thy law. I entreated thy face with all my heart: have mercy on me according to thy word. I have thought on my ways: and turned my feet unto thy testimonies. I am ready, and am not troubled: that I may keep thy commandments. The cords of the wicked have encompassed me: but I have not forgotten thy law. I rose at midnight to give praise to thee; for the judgments of thy justification. I am a partaker with all them that fear thee, and that keep thy commandments. The earth, O LORD, is full of thy mercy: teach me thy justifications.

TETH. Thou hast done well with thy servant, O LORD, according to thy word. Teach me goodness and discipline and knowledge; for I have believed thy commandments. Before I was humbled I offended; therefore have I kept thy word. Thou art good; and in thy goodness teach me thy justifications. The iniquity of the proud hath been multiplied over me: but I will seek thy commandments with my whole heart. Their heart is curdled like milk: but I have meditated on thy law. It is good for me that thou hast humbled me, that I may learn thy justifications. The law of thy mouth is good to me, above thousands of gold and silver.

JOD. Thy hands have made me and formed me: give me understanding, and I will learn thy commandments. They that fear thee shall see me, and shall be glad: because I have greatly hoped in thy words. I know, O LORD, that thy judgments are equity: and in thy truth thou hast humbled me. O! let thy mercy be for my comfort, according to thy word unto thy servant. Let thy tender mercies come unto me, and I shall live: for thy law is my meditation. Let the proud be ashamed, because they have done unjustly towards me: but I will be employed in thy commandments. Let them that fear thee turn to me and they that know thy testimonies. Let my heart be undefiled in thy justifications, that I may not be confounded.

CAPH. My soul hath fainted after thy salvation: and in thy word I have very much hoped. My eyes have failed for thy word, saying: When wilt thou comfort me? For I am become like a bottle in the frost: I have not forgotten thy justifications. How many are the days of thy servant: when wilt thou execute judgment on them that persecute me? The wicked have told me fables: but not as thy law. All thy statutes are truth: they have persecuted me unjustly, do thou help me. They had almost made an end of me upon earth: but I have not forsaken thy commandments. Quicken thou me according to thy mercy: and I shall keep the testimonies of thy mouth.

LAMED. Forever, O LORD, thy word standeth firm in heaven. Thy truth unto all generations: thou hast founded the earth, and it continueth. By thy ordinance the day goeth on: for all things serve thee. Unless thy law had been my meditation, I had then perhaps perished in my abjection. Thy justifications I will never forget: for by them thou hast given me life. I am thine, save thou me: for I have sought thy justifications. The wicked have waited for me to destroy me: but I have understood thy testimonies. I have seen an end to all persecution: thy commandment is exceeding broad.

MEM. O how have I loved thy law, O LORD! it is my meditation all the day. Through thy commandment, thou hast made me wiser than my enemies: for it is ever with me. I have understood more than all my teachers: because thy testimonies are my meditation. I have had understanding above ancients: because I have sought thy commandments. I have restrained my feet from every evil way: that I may keep thy words. I have not declined from thy judgments, because thou hast set me a law. How sweet are thy words to my palate! more than honey to my mouth. By thy commandments I have had understanding: therefore have I hated every way of iniquity.

NUN. Thy word is a lamp to my feet, and a light to my paths. I have sworn and am determined to keep the judgments of thy justice. I have been humbled, O LORD, exceedingly: quicken thou me according to thy word. The free offerings of my mouth make acceptable, O LORD: and teach me thy judgments. My soul is continually in my hands: and I have not forgotten thy law. Sinners have laid a snare for me: but I have not erred from thy precepts. I have purchased thy testimonies for an inheritance forever: because they are a joy to my heart. I have inclined my heart to do thy justifications forever, for the reward.

SAMECH. I have hated the unjust: and have loved thy law. Thou art my helper and my protector: and in thy word I have greatly hoped. Depart from me, ye malignant: and I will search the commandments of my God. Uphold me according to thy word, and I shall live: and let me not be confounded in my expectation. Help me, and I shall be saved: and I will meditate always on thy justifications. Thou hast despised all them that fall off from thy judgments; for their thought is unjust. I have accounted all the sinners of the earth prevaricators: therefore have I loved thy testimonies. Pierce thou my flesh with thy fear: for I am afraid of thy judgments.

AIN. I have done judgment and justice: give me not up to them that slander me. Uphold thy servant unto good: let not the proud calumniate me. My eyes have fainted after thy salvation: and for the word of thy justice. Deal with thy servant according to thy mercy: and teach me thy justifications. I am thy servant: give me understanding that I may know thy testimonies. It is time, O LORD, to do: they have dissipated thy law. Therefore have I loved thy commandments above gold and the topaz. Therefore was I directed to all thy commandments: I have hated all wicked ways.

PHE. Thy testimonies are wonderful: therefore my soul hath sought them. The declaration of thy words giveth light: and giveth understanding to little ones. I opened my mouth and panted: because I longed for thy commandments. Look thou upon me, and have mercy on me, according to the judgment of them that love thy name. Direct my steps according to thy word: and let no iniquity have dominion over me. Redeem me from the calumnies of men: that I may keep thy commandments. Make thy face to shine upon thy servant: and teach me thy justifications. My eyes have sent forth springs of water: because they have not kept thy law.

SADE. Thou art just, O LORD: and thy judgment is right. Thou hast commanded justice thy testimonies: and thy truth exceedingly. My zeal hath made me pine away: because my enemies forgot thy words. Thy word is exceedingly refined: and thy servant hath loved it. I am very young and despised; but I forgot not thy justifications. Thy justice is justice for ever: and thy law is the truth. Trouble and anguish have found me: thy commandments are my meditation. Thy testimonies are justice for ever: give me understanding, and I shall live.

COPH. I cried with my whole heart, hear me, O LORD: I will seek thy justifications. I cried unto thee, save me: that I may keep thy commandments. I prevented the dawning of the day, and cried: because in thy words I very much hoped. My eyes to thee have prevented the morning: that I might meditate on thy words. Hear thou my voice, O LORD, according to thy mercy: and quicken me according to thy mercy. They that persecute me have drawn nigh to iniquity; but they are gone far off from thy law. Thou art near, O LORD: and all thy ways are truth. I have known from the beginning concerning thy testimonies: that thou hast founded them forever.

RES. See my humiliation and deliver me: for I have not forgotten thy law. Judge my judgment and redeem me: quicken thou me for thy word's sake. Salvation is far from sinners; because they have not sought thy justifications. Many, O LORD, are thy mercies: quicken me according to thy judgment. Many are they that persecute me, and afflict me; but I have not declined from thy testimonies. I beheld the transgressors, and I pined away; because they kept not thy word. Behold I have loved thy commandments, O LORD; quicken me thou in thy mercy. The beginning of thy words is truth: all the judgments of thy justice are forever.

SIN. Princes have persecuted me without cause: and my heart hath been in awe of thy words. I will rejoice at thy words, as one that hath found great spoil. I have hated and abhorred iniquity; but I have loved thy law. Seven times a day I have given praise to thee, for the judgments of thy justice. Much peace have they that love thy law, and to them there is no stumbling block. I looked to thy salvation, O LORD: and I loved thy commandments. My soul hath kept thy testimonies: and hath loved them exceedingly. I have kept thy commandments and thy testimonies: because all my ways are in thy sight.

TAU. Let my supplication, O LORD, come near in thy sight: give me understanding according to thy word. Let my request come in before thee; deliver thou me according to thy word. My lips shall utter a hymn, when thou shalt teach me thy justifications. My tongue shall pronounce thy word: because all thy commandments are justice. Let thy hand be with me to save me; for I have chosen thy precepts. I have longed for thy salvation, O LORD; and thy law is my meditation. My soul shall live and shall praise thee: and thy judgments shall help me. I have gone astray like a sheep that is lost: seek thy servant, because I have not forgotten thy commandments.

135

Confitemini Domino

Praise the LORD, for he is good: for his mercy endureth forever. Praise ye the God of gods: for his mercy endureth forever. Praise ye the LORD of lords: for his mercy endureth forever. Who alone doth great wonders: for his mercy endureth forever. Who made the heavens in understanding: for his mercy endureth forever. Who established the earth above the waters: for his mercy endureth forever. Who made the great lights: for his mercy endureth forever. The sun to rule over the day: for his mercy endureth forever. The moon and the stars to rule the night: for his mercy endureth forever. Who smote Egypt with their firstborn: for his mercy endureth forever. Who brought out Israel from among them: for his mercy endureth forever. With a mighty hand and a stretched out arm: for his mercy endureth forever. Who divided the Red Sea into parts: for his mercy endureth forever. And brought out Israel through the midst thereof: for his mercy endureth forever. And overthrew Pharaoh and his host in the Red Sea: for his mercy endureth forever. Who led his people through the desert: for his mercy endureth forever. Who smote great kings: for his mercy endureth forever. And slew strong kings: for his mercy endureth forever. Sehon king of the Amorrhites: for his mercy endureth forever. And Og king of Basan: for his mercy endureth forever. And he gave their land for an inheritance: for his mercy endureth forever. For an inheritance to his servant Israel: for his mercy endureth forever. For he was mindful of us in our affliction: for his mercy endureth forever. And he redeemed us from our enemies: for his mercy endureth forever. Who giveth food to all flesh: for his mercy endureth forever. Give glory to the God of heaven: for his mercy endureth forever. Give glory to the LORD of lords: for his mercy endureth forever.

136

Super flumina

Upon the rivers of Babylon, there we sat and wept: when we remembered Zion: On the willows in the midst thereof we hung up our instruments. For there they that led us into captivity required of us the words of songs. And they that carried us away, said: Sing ye to us a hymn of the songs of Sion. How shall we sing the song of the LORD in a strange land? If I forget thee, O Jerusalem, let my right hand be forgotten. Let my tongue cleave to my jaws, if I do not remember thee: If I make not Jerusalem the beginning of my joy. Remember, O Lord, the children of Edom, in the day of Jerusalem: Who say: Rase it, rase it, even to the foundation thereof. O daughter of Babylon, miserable: blessed shall he be who shall repay thee thy payment which thou hast paid us. Blessed be he that shall take and dash thy little ones against the rock.

Session Ten

137

Confitebor tibi

I will praise thee, O LORD, with my whole heart: for thou hast heard the words of my mouth. I will sing praise to thee in the sight of his angels: I will worship towards thy holy temple, and I will give glory to thy name. For thy mercy, and for thy truth: for thou hast magnified thy holy name above all. In what day soever I shall call upon thee, hear me: thou shall multiply strength in my soul. May all the kings of the earth give glory to thee: for they have heard all the words of thy mouth. And let them sing in the ways of the LORD: for great is the glory of the LORD. For the LORD is high, and looketh on the low: and the high he knoweth afar off. If I shall walk in the midst of tribulation, thou wilt quicken me: and thou hast stretched forth thy hand against the wrath of my enemies: and thy right hand hath saved me. The LORD will repay for me: thy mercy, O LORD, endureth forever: O despise not the work of thy hands.

138

Domine, probasti

LORD, thou hast proved me, and known me: Thou hast known my sitting down, and my rising up. Thou hast understood my thoughts afar off: my path and my line thou hast searched out. And thou hast foreseen all my ways: for there is no speech in my tongue. Behold, O LORD, thou hast known all things, the last and those of old: thou hast formed me, and hast laid thy hand upon me. Thy knowledge is become wonderful to me: it is high, and I cannot reach to it. Whither shall I go from thy spirit? or whither shall I flee from thy face? If I ascend into heaven, thou art there: if I descend into hell, thou art present. If I take my wings early in the morning, and dwell in the uttermost parts of the sea: Even there also shall thy hand lead me: and thy right hand shall hold me. And I said: Perhaps darkness shall cover me: and night shall be my light in my pleasures. But darkness shall not be dark to thee, and night shall be light as day: the darkness thereof, and the light thereof are alike to thee. For thou hast possessed my reins: thou hast protected me from my mother's womb. I will praise thee, for thou art fearfully magnified: wonderful are thy works, and my soul knoweth right well. My bone is not hidden from thee, which thou hast made in secret: and my substance in the lower parts of the earth. Thy eyes did see my imperfect being, and in thy book all shall be written: days shall be formed, and no one in them. But to me thy friends, O God, are made exceedingly honourable: their principality is exceedingly strengthened. I will number them, and they shall be multiplied above the sand: I rose up and am still with thee. If thou wilt kill the wicked, O God: ye men of blood, depart from me: Because you say in thought: They shall receive thy cities in vain. Have I not hated them, O LORD, that hated thee: and pine away because of thy enemies? I have hated them with a perfect hatred: and they are become enemies to me. Prove me, O God, and know my heart: examine me, and know my paths. And see if there be in me the way of iniquity: and lead me in the eternal way.

139

Eripe me, Domine

Deliver me, O LORD, from the evil man: rescue me from the unjust man. Who have devised iniquities in their hearts: all the day long they designed battles. They have sharpened their tongues like a serpent: the venom of asps is under their lips. Keep me, O LORD, from the hand of the wicked: and from unjust men deliver me. Who have proposed to supplant my steps. The proud have hidden a net for me. And they have stretched out cords for a snare: they have laid for me a stumbling block by the wayside. I said to the LORD: Thou art my God: hear, O LORD, the voice of my supplication. O LORD, LORD, the strength of my salvation: thou hast overshadowed my head in the day of battle. Give me not up, O LORD, from my desire to the wicked: they have plotted against me; do not thou forsake me, lest they should triumph. The head of them compassing me about: the labour of their lips shall overwhelm them. Burning coals shall fall upon them; thou wilt cast them down into the fire: in miseries they shall not be able to stand. A man full of tongue shall not be established in the earth: evil shall catch the unjust man unto destruction. I know that the LORD will do justice to the needy, and will revenge the poor. But as for the just, they shall give glory to thy name: and the upright shall dwell with thy countenance.

140

Domine, clamavi

I have cried to thee, O LORD, hear me: hearken to my voice, when I cry to thee. Let my prayer be directed as incense in thy sight; the lifting up of my hands, as evening sacrifice. Set a watch, O LORD, before my mouth: and a door round about my lips. Incline not my heart to evil words; to make excuses in sins. With men that work iniquity: and I will not communicate with the choicest of them. The just shall correct me in mercy, and shall reprove me: but let not the oil of the sinner fatten my head. For my prayer also shall still be against the things with which they are well pleased: Their judges falling upon the rock have been swallowed up. They shall hear my words, for they have prevailed: As when the thickness of the earth is broken up upon the ground: Our bones are scattered by the side of hell. But o to thee, O LORD, LORD, are my eyes: in thee have I put my trust, take not away my soul. Keep me from the snare, which they have laid for me, and from the stumbling blocks of them that work iniquity. The wicked shall fall in his net: I am alone until I pass.

141

Voce mea

I cried to the LORD with my voice: with my voice I made supplication to the LORD. In his sight I pour out my prayer, and before him I declare my trouble: When my spirit failed me, then thou knewest my paths. In this way wherein I walked, they have hidden a snare for me. I looked on my right hand, and beheld, and there was no one that would know me. Flight hath failed me: and there is no one that hath regard to my soul. I cried to thee, O LORD: I said: Thou art my hope, my portion in the land of the living. Attend to my supplication: for I am brought very low. Deliver me from my persecutors; for they are stronger than I. Bring my soul out of prison, that I may praise thy name: the just wait for me, until thou reward me.

142

Domine, exaudi

Hear, O LORD, my prayer: give ear to my supplication in thy truth: hear me in thy justice. And enter not into judgment with thy servant: for in thy sight no man living shall be justified. For the enemy hath persecuted my soul: he hath brought down my life to the earth. He hath made me to dwell in darkness as those that have been dead of old: And my spirit is in anguish within me: my heart within me is troubled. I remembered the days of old, I meditated on all thy works: I meditated upon the works of thy hands. I stretched forth my hands to thee: my soul is as earth without water unto thee. Hear me speedily, O LORD: my spirit hath fainted away. Turn not away thy face from me, lest I be like unto them that go down into the pit. Cause me to hear thy mercy in the morning; for in thee have I hoped. Make the way known to me, wherein I should walk: for I have lifted up my soul to thee. Deliver me from my enemies, O LORD, to thee have I fled: Teach me to do thy will, for thou art my God. Thy good spirit shall lead me into the right land: For thy name's sake, O LORD, thou wilt quicken me in thy justice. Thou wilt bring my soul out of trouble: And in thy mercy thou wilt destroy my enemies. And thou wilt cut off all them that afflict my soul: for I am thy servant.

143

Benedictus Dominus

Blessed be the LORD my God, who teacheth my hands to fight, and my fingers to war. My mercy, and my refuge: my support, and my deliverer: My protector, and I have hoped in him: who subdueth my people under me. LORD, what is man, that thou art made known to him? or the son of man, that thou makest account of him? Man is like to vanity: his days pass away like a shadow. LORD, bow down thy heavens and descend: touch the mountains and they shall smoke. Send forth lightning, and thou shalt scatter them: shoot out thy arrows, and thou shalt trouble them. Put forth thy hand from on high, take me out, and deliver me from many waters: from the hand of strange children: Whose mouth hath spoken vanity: and their right hand is the right hand of iniquity. To thee, O God, I will sing a new canticle: on the psaltery and an instrument of ten strings I will sing praises to thee. Who givest salvation to kings: who hast redeemed thy servant David from the malicious sword: Deliver me, And rescue me out of the hand of strange children; whose mouth hath spoken vanity: and their right hand is the right hand of iniquity: Whose sons are as new plants in their youth: Their daughters decked out, adorned round about after the similitude of a temple: Their storehouses full, flowing out of this into that. Their sheep fruitful in young, abounding in their goings forth: Their oxen fat. There is no breach of wall, nor passage, nor crying out in their streets. They have called the people happy, that hath these things: but happy is that people whose God is the LORD.

144

Exaltabo te, Deus

I will extol thee, O God my king: and I will bless thy name for ever; yea, for ever and ever. Every day I will bless thee: and I will praise thy name for ever; yea, for ever and ever. Great is the LORD, and greatly to be praised: and of his greatness there is no end. Generation and generation shall praise thy works: and they shall declare thy power. They shall speak of the magnificence of the glory of thy holiness: and shall tell thy wondrous works. And they shall speak of the might of thy terrible acts: and shall declare thy greatness. They shall publish the memory of the abundance of thy sweetness: and shall rejoice in thy justice. The LORD is gracious and merciful: patient and plenteous in mercy. The LORD is sweet to all: and his tender mercies are over all his works. Let all thy works, O LORD, praise thee: and let thy saints bless thee. They shall speak of the glory of thy kingdom: and shall tell of thy power: To make thy might known to the sons of men: and the glory of the magnificence of thy kingdom. Thy kingdom is a kingdom of all ages: and thy dominion endureth throughout all generations. The LORD is faithful in all his words: and holy in all his works. The LORD lifteth up all that fall: and setteth up all that are cast down. The eyes of all hope in thee, O LORD: and thou givest them meat in due season. Thou openest thy hand, and fillest with blessing every living creature. The LORD is just in all his ways: and holy in all his works. The LORD is nigh unto all them that call upon him: to all that call upon him in truth. He will do the will of them that fear him: and he will hear their prayer, and save them. The LORD keepeth all them that love him; but all the wicked he will destroy. My mouth shall speak the praise of the LORD: and let all flesh bless thy holy name forever; yea, forever and ever.

145

Lauda, anima

Praise the LORD, O my soul, in my life I will praise the LORD: I will sing to my God as long as I shall be. Put not your trust in princes: In the children of men, in whom there is no salvation. His spirit shall go forth, and he shall return into his earth: in that day all their thoughts shall perish. Blessed is he who hath the God of Jacob for his helper, whose hope is in the LORD his God: Who made heaven and earth, the sea, and all things that are in them. Who keepeth truth forever: who executeth judgment for them that suffer wrong: who giveth food to the hungry. The LORD looseth them that are fettered: The LORD enlighteneth the blind. The LORD lifteth up them that are cast down: the LORD loveth the just. The Lord keepeth the strangers, he will support the fatherless and the widow: and the ways of sinners he will destroy. The LORD shall reign forever: thy God, O Zion, unto generation and generation.

146

Laudate Dominum

Praise ye the LORD, because psalm is good: to our God be joyful and comely praise. The LORD buildeth up Jerusalem: he will gather together the dispersed of Israel. Who healeth the broken of heart, and bindeth up their bruises. Who telleth the number of the stars: and calleth them all by their names. Great is our LORD, and great is his power: and of his wisdom there is no number. The LORD lifteth up the meek, and bringeth the wicked down even to the ground. Sing ye to the LORD with praise: sing to our God upon the harp. Who covereth the heaven with clouds, and prepareth rain for the earth. Who maketh grass to grow on the mountains, and herbs for the service of men. Who giveth to beasts their food: and to the young ravens that call upon him. He shall not delight in the strength of the horse: nor take pleasure in the legs of a man. The LORD taketh pleasure in them that fear him: and in them that hope in his mercy.

God, make speed to save us. LORD, make haste to help us.

Glory to the Father, and to the Son, and to the Holy Spirit, now and ever, and unto ages of ages. Amen.

A Collect for After the Psalms

Let angels, virtues, stars, powers, praise you, O LORD. Let those things which owe you their origin give service and exult you in praise, that they may sing to you in harmony with the universe, and that your will may be done on earth as it is in heaven. Let your favor be upon your people, we pray. O LORD, that by exulting you with our joined forces, we may remain as one, armed with your Word which you speak, and our lives always contemplating your truth and salvation, which you have shown in your surpassing greatness. We praise you, O LORD. We display our praise with thanks. We praise you with lute and harp, with drum and dance, with strings and pipe, with sounding cymbals, that we may always receive your mercy, O Christ, Savior of the world; who reigns with the Father and the Holy Spirit, now and ever, and unto the ages of ages. Amen.

Hymn

Glory Be to God

Gloria in Excelsis Deo

FROM THE BOOK OF COMMON PRAYER, 1892

Glory be to God on high
And in earth peace, goodwill towards men,
We praise thee, we bless thee,
we worship thee, we glorify thee,
we give thanks to thee, for thy great glory
O LORD God, heavenly King,
God the Father Almighty.
O LORD, the only-begotten Son, Jesu Christ;
O LORD God, Lamb of God, Son of the Father,
that takest away the sins of the world,
have mercy upon us.
Thou that takest away the sins of the world,
have mercy upon us.
Thou that takest away the sins of the world,
receive our prayer.
Thou that sittest at the right hand of God the Father,
have mercy upon us.
For thou only art holy;
thou only art the LORD;
thou only, O Christ,
with the Holy Ghost,
art most high
in the glory of God the Father. Amen.

For Sundays

Thee, O God, we praise

Te Deum laudamus

FROM THE BOOK OF COMMON PRAYER, 1892

We praise thee, O God: we acknowledge thee to be the Lord.

All the earth doth worship thee: the Father everlasting.

To thee all Angels cry aloud: the Heavens, and all the Powers therein.

To thee Cherubim and Seraphim: continually do cry,

Holy, Holy, Holy: LORD God of Sabaoth;

Heaven and earth are full of the Majesty: of thy glory.

The glorious company of the Apostles: praise thee.

The goodly fellowship of the Prophets: praise thee.

The noble army of Martyrs: praise thee.

The holy Church throughout all the world: doth acknowledge thee;

The Father: of an infinite Majesty;

Thine honourable, true: and only Son;

Also the Holy Ghost: the Comforter.

Thou art the King of Glory: O Christ.

Thou art the everlasting Son: of the Father.

When thou tookest upon thee to deliver man: thou didst not abhor
the Virgin's womb.

When thou hadst overcome the sharpness of death: thou didst open
the Kingdom of Heaven to all believers.

Thou sittest at the right hand of God: in the glory of the Father.

We believe that thou shalt come: to be our Judge.

We therefore pray thee, help thy servants: whom thou hast redeemed
with thy precious blood.

Make them to be numbered with thy Saints: in glory everlasting.

O LORD, save thy people: and bless thine heritage.

Govern them: and lift them up for ever.

Day by day: we magnify thee;

And we worship thy Name: ever world without end.

Vouchsafe, O LORD: to keep us this day without sin.

O LORD, have mercy upon us: have mercy upon us.

O LORD, let thy mercy lighten upon us: as our trust is in thee.

O LORD, in thee have I trusted: let me never be confounded.

A Collect for After the Hymn

Look down, O LORD, at our prayers, you who visits feeble humans, and bestow on us your sanctification and immortality, O Christ, who reigns with the Father and the Holy Spirit, now and ever, and unto the ages of ages. Amen.

Gospel

The Gospel According to St. Luke

LUKE 24:1–8

But on the first day of the week, at early in the morning, they came to the sepulcher, bringing the spices which they had prepared. They found the stone rolled back from the sepulcher, but going in, they did not find the body of the LORD Jesus. It came to pass, as they were astonished in their mind at this, behold, two men stood by them, in shining apparel. The women were afraid and bowed down their countenance towards the ground, but the men said to them, "Why do you seek the living among the dead? He is not here but has risen." Remember how he told you, when he was still in Galilee saying that the Son of Man must be delivered into the hands of sinful men, and be crucified, and the third day rise again. Then they remembered his words.

Amen, thanks be to God.

A Collect for After the Gospel

May the spiritual songs and delightful hymns we sing to you, O Christ, please your majesty, as we offer our spiritual sacrifice; who lives and reigns with the eternal living Father and the Holy Spirit, now and ever, and unto the ages of ages. Amen.

Another

In the light of dawn, with the risen Creator, let us rejoice in the LORD, who conquered death, where we may be able to look over our sins, and let us walk in the newness of life, who lives and reigns with the eternal living Father and the Holy Spirit, now and ever, and unto the ages of ages. Amen.

A Collect for After the Gospel on Sundays

In the morning light, Christ was resurrected in accordance with the LORD, subduing death and defeating sin forever. This was done so that we may walk in newness of life, who lives and reigns with the eternal living Father and the Holy Spirit, now and ever, and unto the ages of ages. Amen.

Another

As we worship at the beginning of the LORD's Resurrection, let us bring praise and thanks to our triune God with a united affection, begging of His mercy that we may participate in the blessed Resurrection of our LORD and Savior, both in spirit and in body, who lives and reigns with the living Father and the Holy Spirit, now and ever, and unto the ages of ages. Amen.

Martyrs

For Sundays and Easter

Remember also, O LORD, the names of those who have gone before us with the sign of faith and rest in the sleep of peace, together with all holy and venerable priests who in the whole world offer the spiritual sacrifice to God the Father, and Son, and Holy Spirit, the priest N., head of our house, offers sacrifice for himself and all pertaining to him, and for the company of the whole catholic church; and for commemorating the order of those at rest the venerable patriarchs, prophets, Apostles, and Martyrs, and all Saints also, that they may deign to prevail upon the LORD our God for us.

Saint Stephen, pray for us.

Saint Comgall, pray for us.

Saint Martin, pray for us.

Saint Cainnech, pray for us.

Saint Jerome, pray for us.

Saint Finbar, pray for us.

Saint Augustine, pray for us.

Saint Nessan, pray for us.

Saint Gregory, pray for us.

Saint Fachtna, pray for us.

Saint Hilary, pray for us.

Saint Lua, pray for us.

Saint Patrick, pray for us.

Saint Lacten, pray for us.

Saint Ailbe, pray for us.

Saint Ruadhan, pray for us.

Saint Finnian, pray for us.

Saint Carthage, pray for us.

Saint Finnian, pray for us.

Saint Kevin, pray for us.

Saint Ciaran, pray for us.

Saint Mochoemog, pray for us.

Saint Ciaran, pray for us.

Saint Brigid, pray for us.

Saint Brendan, pray for us.

Saint Ite, pray for us.

Saint Brendan, pray for us.

Saint Scetha, pray for us.

Saint Columba, pray for us.

Saint Sinecha, pray for us.

Saint Columba, pray for us.

Saint Samthann, pray for us.

All you Saints, pray for us.

Be gracious and spare us, O LORD.

Be gracious and free us, O LORD.

From all evil, free us, O LORD.

Through your Cross, Free us, O LORD.

We sinners entreat you, hear us, O Son of God.

We entreat you, hear us, and grant us peace.

We entreat you, hear us.

Lamb of God who takes away the sins of the world,

have mercy on us. Christ hear us.

These are the ones who came out of the great tribulation, washed their robes, and have made them white in the blood of the Lamb.

Another

In remembrance of your martyrs, O LORD, be present at the prayers of your servants, O Christ.

A Collect for the Martyrs

After fires and plates,

crosses and beasts,

Holy with great triumph

Riding in the Kingdom

And in consolation.

Another

Holy and glorious, wonderful yet powerful martyrs, in whose works the LORD and in the congregation rejoice, our best intercessors and strongest protectors, remember us always in the sight of the LORD, that we may earn the aid of the LORD, who reigns with the living Father and the Holy Spirit, now and ever, and unto the ages of ages. Amen.

Common Prayer

Remember not the iniquities of our bygone ways and let your mercy come before us quickly, for we have become exceeding poor.

Help us, O God our Savior, for the glory of your name. LORD, deliver us and forgive our sins for your name's sake. Do not give up to the beasts the soul that confesses to you. Forget not the souls of your poor forever. Look upon your covenant, O LORD, who reigns now and ever, and unto the ages of ages. Amen.

For our sins

O God, come to my aid. O LORD, make haste to help me.

Make haste, O LORD, to deliver us from all our sins, who reigns now and ever, and unto the ages of ages. Amen.

For those to be baptized

Save your people, O LORD, and bless your heritage. Rule them and lift them up forever.

Have mercy, O LORD, on your catholic church, which you have redeemed in your holy blood, who reigns now and ever, and unto the ages of ages. Amen.

For the clergy

Arise, O LORD, and go into your eternal peace, you and the ark of your holiness. Your priests will be clothed with justice and your saints exalted.

Let all your saints rejoice in you, O LORD, who places their hope in you in all truth, now and ever, and unto the ages of ages. Amen.

For the people and their leaders

The LORD will give strength to his people; The LORD blesses his people in peace.

For the martyrs

By the virtue of your eternal name, Almighty God, we pray you to make us companions of martyrs and of all your saints by the merits of your saints, equal in faith, vigorous in devotion, and like in passion, to make us equal in the resurrection of the fortunate, who reigns now and ever, and unto the ages of ages. Amen.

For the penitents

Have mercy on me, O God, your second great mercy.

Grant us, O LORD, pardon to those who ask you out of faith your second great mercy, O God, who reigns now and ever, and unto the ages of ages. Amen.

Symbol of Faith

We believe in God, the Father almighty, unseen, creator of creatures seen and unseen. We believe in Jesus Christ, His only Son, our LORD, almighty God, conceived by the power of the Holy Spirit, born from the Virgin Mary, suffered under Pontius Pilate; who was crucified, died, and was buried; He descended into Hell; on the third day he rose again from the dead; He ascended into heaven, and is seated at the right hand of God the Father Almighty; from there He will come to judge the living and the dead. We believe in the Holy Spirit, almighty God, of one substance with the Father and Son. The holy catholic church, the forgiveness of sins, communion of saints, and the resurrection of the dead. We believe in life after death, and eternal life in the glory of Christ. All these things we believe in God. Amen.

Divine Prayer

As taught by divine instruction and guided by divine institution, we dare to say:

Our Father in heaven, hallowed be your name; your kingdom come, your will be done, on earth as it is in heaven. Give us today our substantial bread. Forgive us our debts as we forgive our debtors. Keep us from falling into temptation and deliver us from evil. Amen.

For yours is the kingdom, and the power, and the glory of the Father, and the Son, and Holy Spirit, now and ever, and unto the ages of ages. Amen.

The Order of Seconde

Invitatory

God, make speed to save us. LORD, make haste to help us.

Glory to the Father, and to the Son, and to the Holy Spirit, now and ever, and unto the ages of ages. Amen.

Hasten, O LORD, to free us from all our sins; for you live and reign with the eternal living Father and the Holy Spirit, now and ever, and unto the ages of ages. Amen.

We have sinned, O LORD, we have sinned, spare us our sins, and save us; you who guided Noah over the flood waves, hear us; who with your word recalled Jonah from the abyss; deliver us; who stretched forth your hand to Peter as he sank, help us, O Christ. Son of God, you accomplished marvelous things of the LORD with our fathers, be favorable in our days also; Stretch forth your hand from on high.

Deliver us, O Christ. Hear us, O Christ. Hear us, O Christ. Hear us, O Lord have mercy.

Son of God, you who did marvelous things of the LORD with our fathers, be favorable in our days also; Stretch forth your hand from on high. Deliver us, O Christ. Hear us, O Christ.

A Collect for the Hour of Seconde

Protect us this day, O LORD, holy Father, almighty and eternal God, and in your compassion and mercy, help us, guide us, and enlighten our hearts. Safeguard, O LORD, our thoughts, speech, and deeds pleasing under your watch, that we may do your will and walk in your righteous path during our lifetime. Amen.

Another

We pray to you, Most High
As the light of the sun has risen
In the name of the rising Christ
Be present with us, O LORD
Who reigns now and ever,
And unto the ages of ages. Amen.

Another

Hear us, O LORD, your suppliant, who at this first hour of the day give you thanks to the LORD our God, who has redeemed us in your holy blood, kindly answer the early prayers and petitions we offer to you, who reigns with you and the Holy Spirit, now and ever, and unto the ages of ages. Amen.

Another

O LORD, holy Father, Almighty eternal God, who makes the day illustrious, have mercy on us. O LORD, restore to us the joy of your salvation, and strengthen us with a perfect spirit, that the morning star may arise in our hearts, through you, Jesus Christ, who reigns with the Father and the Holy Spirit, now and ever, and unto the ages of ages. Amen.

50

Misere mei, Deus

Have mercy on me, O God, according to thy great mercy. And according to the multitude of thy tender mercies blot out my iniquity. Wash me yet more from my iniquity, and cleanse me from my sin. For I know my iniquity, and my sin is always before me. To thee only have I sinned, and have done evil before thee: that thou mayst be justified in thy words and mayst overcome when thou art judged. For behold I was conceived in iniquities; and in sins did my mother conceive me. For behold thou hast loved truth: the uncertain and hidden things of thy wisdom thou hast made manifest to me. Thou shalt sprinkle me with hyssop, and I shall be cleansed: thou shalt wash me, and I shall be made whiter than snow. To my hearing thou shalt give joy and gladness: and the bones that have been humbled shall rejoice. Turn away thy face from my sins, and blot out all my iniquities. Create a clean heart in me, O God: and renew a right spirit within my bowels. Cast me not away from thy face; and take not thy holy spirit from me. Restore unto me the joy of thy salvation, and strengthen me with a perfect spirit. I will teach the unjust thy ways: and the wicked shall be converted to thee. Deliver me from blood, O God, thou God of my salvation: and my tongue shall extol thy justice. O LORD, thou wilt open my lips: and my mouth shall declare thy praise. For if thou hadst desired sacrifice, I would indeed have given it: with burnt offerings thou wilt not be delighted. A sacrifice to God is an afflicted spirit: a contrite and humbled heart, O God, thou wilt not despise. Deal favourably, O LORD, in thy good will with Zion; that the walls of Jerusalem may be built up. Then shalt thou accept the sacrifice of justice, oblations and whole burnt offerings: then shall they lay calves upon thy altar.

62

Deus, Deus meus

O God, my God, to thee do I watch at break of day. For thee my soul hath thirsted; for thee my flesh, O how many ways! In a desert land, and where there is no way, and no water: so in the sanctuary have I come before thee, to see thy power and thy glory. For thy mercy is better than lives: thee my lips shall praise. Thus will I bless thee all my life long: and in thy name I will lift up my hands. Let my soul be filled as with marrow and fatness: and my mouth shall praise thee with joyful lips. If I have remembered thee upon my bed, I will meditate on thee in the morning: Because thou hast been my helper. And I will rejoice under the covert of thy wings: My soul hath stuck close to thee: thy right hand hath received me. But they have sought my soul in vain, they shall go into the lower parts of the earth: They shall be delivered into the hands of the sword, they shall be the portions of foxes.

But the king shall rejoice in God, all they shall be praised that swear by him: because the mouth is stopped of them that speak wicked things.

Psalm 89 Antiphons for Sunday

From this day the night is diminished and the day increases, the darkness shakes and the light increases, the losses of the night are brought over to the gain of the light.

Another

Turn back, O LORD, for how long? Let your servants entreat you.

Another

May the brightness of the LORD our God be upon us.

89

Domine, refugium

Before the mountains were made, or the earth and the world was formed; from eternity and to eternity thou art God. Turn not man away to be brought low: and thou hast said: Be converted, O ye sons of men. For a thousand years in thy sight are as yesterday, which is past. And as a watch in the night, Things that are counted nothing, shall their years be. In the morning man shall grow up like grass; in the morning he shall flourish and pass away: in the evening he shall fall, grow dry, and wither. For in thy wrath we have fainted away: and are troubled in thy indignation. Thou hast set our iniquities before thy eyes: our life in the light of thy countenance. For all our days are spent; and in thy wrath we have fainted away. Our years shall be considered as a spider: The days of our years in them are threescore and ten years. But if in the strong they be fourscore years: and what is more of them is labour and sorrow. For mildness is come upon us: and we shall be corrected. Who knoweth the power of thy anger, and for thy fear can number thy wrath? So make thy right hand known: and men learned in heart, in wisdom. Return, O LORD, how long? and be entreated in favour of thy servants. We are filled in the morning with thy mercy: and we have rejoiced, and are delighted all our days. We have rejoiced for the days in which thou hast humbled us: for the years in which we have seen evils. Look upon thy servants and upon their works: and direct their children. And let the brightness of the LORD our God be upon us: and direct thou the works of our hands over us; yea, the work of our hands do thou direct.

God, make speed to save us. LORD, make haste to help us.

Glory to the Father, and to the Son, and to the Holy Spirit, now and ever, and unto the ages of ages. Amen.

A Collect for After the Psalms

Most High God, king of the angels,

O God, praise of all elements,

O God, glory and joy of the saints,

Guard the souls of your servants,

Who reigns now and ever,

And unto the ages of ages. Amen.

Hymn

Here may be sung a canticle or hymn.

A Collect for After the Hymn

Look down, O LORD, at our prayers, you who visits feeble humans, and bestow on us your sanctification and immortality, O Christ, who reigns with you and the Holy Spirit, now and ever, and unto the ages of ages. Amen.

Another

The light has risen in the first light, as it was made at the beginning of the ancient of days. Your only begotten Son, O LORD, who came to cleanse our sins through the cross, who lives with the eternal living Father and the Holy Spirit, now and ever, and unto the ages of ages. Amen.

Gospel

The Gospel According to Saint John

JOHN 1:1–17

In the beginning was the Word, and the Word was with God, and the Word was God. He was in the beginning with God. All things were made by him, and without him nothing was made. In him was life, and the life was the light of men. The light shines in darkness, and the darkness did not comprehend it. There was a man sent from God, whose name was John. He came as a witness, to give testimony of the light, that all men might believe through him. He was not the light but was to give testimony of the light. That was the true light, which enlightens every man that comes into this world. He was in the world, and the world was made by him, and the world knew him not. He came unto his own, and his own received him not. But as many as received him, he gave them power to be made the sons of God, to them that believe in his name. Who are born, not of blood, nor of the will of the flesh, nor of the will of man, but of God. And the Word was made flesh and dwelt among us, (and we saw his glory, the glory as it were of the only begotten of the Father), full of grace and truth. John bore witness of him, and cried out, "This was he of whom I spoke, 'He that shall come after me, is preferred before me because he was before me.'" And from his fullness we all have received, and grace upon grace. For the law was given by Moses; grace and truth came through Jesus Christ.

Amen, thanks be to God.

A Collect for After the Gospel

May the spiritual songs and delightful hymns we sing to you, O Christ, please your majesty, as we offer our spiritual sacrifice; who lives and reigns with the eternal living Father and the Holy Spirit, now and ever, and unto the ages of ages. Amen.

Common Prayer

I put my trust in you, O LORD; let me never be confounded. Deliver me in your justice and rescue me.

O LORD my God, do not depart from me; Attend to my help, O LORD of my salvation.

God, make speed to save us. LORD, make haste to help us.

Make haste, O LORD, to deliver us from all our sins, who reigns with you and the Holy Spirit, now and ever, and unto the ages of ages. Amen.

Protect us, O LORD, as the pupil of your eye, protect us under the shadow of your wings.

Deign to protect and sanctify us all, Almighty God, who reigns with the Father and the Holy Spirit, now and ever, and unto the ages of ages. Amen.

Symbol of Faith

We believe in God, the Father almighty, unseen, creator of creatures seen and unseen. We believe in Jesus Christ, His only Son, our LORD, almighty God, conceived by the power of the Holy Spirit, born from the Virgin Mary, suffered under Pontius Pilate; who was crucified, died, and was buried; He descended into Hell; on the third day he rose again from the dead; He ascended into heaven, and is seated at the right hand of God the Father Almighty; from there He will come to judge the living and the dead. We believe in the Holy Spirit, almighty God, of one substance with the Father and Son. The holy catholic church, the forgiveness of sins, communion of saints, and the resurrection of the dead. We believe in life after death, and eternal life in the glory of Christ. All these things we believe in God. Amen.

Divine Prayer

As taught by divine instruction and guided by divine institution, we dare to say:

Our Father in heaven, hallowed be your name; your kingdom come, your will be done, on earth as it is in heaven. Give us today our substantial bread.

Forgive us our debts as we forgive our debtors. Keep us from falling into temptation and deliver us from evil. Amen.

For yours is the kingdom, and the power, and the glory of the Father, and the Son, and Holy Spirit, now and ever, and unto the ages of ages. Amen.

The Order of Terce

Invitatory

God, make speed to save us. LORD, make haste to help us.

Glory to the Father, and to the Son, and to the Holy Spirit, now and ever, and unto the ages of ages. Amen.

Hasten, O LORD, to free us from all our sins; for you live and reign with the eternal living Father and the Holy Spirit, now and ever, and unto the ages of ages. Amen.

We have sinned, O LORD, we have sinned, spare us our sins, and save us; you who guided Noah over the flood waves, hear us; who with your word recalled Jonah from the abyss; deliver us; who stretched forth your hand to Peter as he sank, help us, O Christ. Son of God, you accomplished marvelous things of the LORD with our fathers, be favorable in our days also; Stretch forth your hand from on high.

Deliver us, O Christ. Hear us, O Christ. Hear us, O Christ. Hear us, O Lord have mercy.

Son of God, you who did marvelous things of the LORD with our fathers, be favorable in our days also; Stretch forth your hand from on high. Deliver us, O Christ. Hear us, O Christ.

A Collect for the Hour of Terce

O Christ, at the third hour
We pray for your mercy
That we may offer
Perpetual thanks;

Who reigns now and ever,
And unto the ages of ages. Amen.

Another

We pray to you, Christ our LORD, who at the third hour of the day sent forth the Holy Spirit while the apostles were praying. May we request to participate in the same grace, who reigns with the Father and the Holy Spirit, now and ever, and unto the ages of ages. Amen.

46

Omnes gentes, plaudite

O clap your hands, all ye nations: shout unto God with the voice of Joy, For the LORD is high, terrible: a great king over all the earth. He hath subdued the people under us; and the nations under our feet. He hath chosen for us his inheritance the beauty of Jacob which he hath loved. God is ascended with jubilee, and the Lord with the sound of trumpet. Sing praises to our God, sing ye: sing praises to our king, sing ye. For God is the king of all the earth: sing ye wisely. God shall reign over the nations: God sitteth on his holy throne. The princes of the people are gathered together, with the God of Abraham: for the strong gods of the earth are exceedingly exalted.

53

Deus, in nomine

When the men of Ziph had come and said to Saul: Is not David hidden with us? Save me, O God, by thy name, and judge me in thy strength. O God, hear my prayer: give ear to the words of my mouth. For strangers have risen up against me; and the mighty have sought after my soul: and they have not set God before their eyes. For behold God is my helper: and the LORD is the protector of my soul. Turn back the evils upon my enemies; and cut them off in thy truth. I will freely sacrifice to thee, and will give praise, O God, to thy name: because it is good: For thou hast delivered me out of all trouble: and my eye hath looked down upon my enemies.

114

Dilexi, quoniam

I have loved, because the LORD will hear the voice of my prayer. Because he hath inclined his ear unto me: and in my days I will call upon him. The sorrows of death have encompassed me: and the perils of hell have found me. I met with trouble and sorrow: And I called upon the name of the LORD. O LORD, deliver my soul. The LORD is merciful and just, and our God sheweth mercy. The LORD is the keeper of little ones: I was little and he delivered me. Turn, O my soul, into thy rest: for the LORD hath been bountiful to thee. For he hath delivered my soul from death: my eyes from tears, my feet from falling. I will please the LORD in the land of the living.

God, make speed to save us. LORD, make haste to help us.

Glory to the Father, and to the Son, and to the Holy Spirit, now and ever, and unto the ages of ages. Amen.

A Collect for after the Psalms

Most High God, king of the angels,

God, praise of all elements,

God, glory and joy of the saints,

Guard the souls of your servants,

Who reigns now and ever,

And unto the ages of ages. Amen.

Hymn

Here may be sung a canticle or hymn.

A Collect for After the Hymn

Look down, O LORD, at our prayers, you who visits feeble humans, and bestow on us your sanctification and immortality, O Christ, who reigns with the Father and the Holy Spirit, now and ever, and unto the ages of ages. Amen.

Gospel

The Gospel According to Acts

ACTS 2:1-15

When the day of the Pentecost had come, they were all together in one place. And suddenly there came a sound from heaven, as of a mighty wind coming, and it filled the whole house where they were sitting. And there appeared to them parted tongues as it were of fire, and it sat upon every one of them. They were all filled with the Holy Spirit, and they began to speak in diverse languages, as the Holy Spirit gave them ability. Now there were devout Jews from every nation under heaven dwelling in Jerusalem. And at this sound, the multitude came together and were confounded in mind, because that every man heard them speaking in the native language of each. Amazed and astonished, they asked, "Are not all these who are speaking Galileans? And how is it we hear, each of us, our own tongue wherein we were born? Parthians, Medes, Elamites, and inhabitants of Mesopotamia, Judea, and Cappadocia, Pontus and Asia, Phrygia, and Pamphylia, Egypt, and the parts of Libya belonging to Cyrene, and strangers from Rome, both Jews and proselytes, Cretans and Arabs, we have heard them speak in our own tongues about the wonderful works of God. They were all astonished, and wondered, saying one to another, "What does this mean?" But others mocked them, saying, "These men are full of new wine." But Peter, standing up with the eleven, lifted up his voice and spoke to them, "Men of Judea and all you that dwell in Jerusalem, let this be known to you, and with your ears receive my words. For these are not drunk, as you suppose, seeing it is but the third hour of the day."

Amen, thanks be to God.

A Collect for After the Gospel

May the spiritual songs and delightful hymns we sing to you, O Christ, please your majesty, as we offer our spiritual sacrifice; who lives and reigns with the eternal living Father and the Holy Spirit, now and ever, and unto the ages of ages. Amen.

Common Prayer

I put my trust in you, O LORD; let me never be confounded. Deliver me in your justice and rescue me.

O LORD my God, do not depart from me; Attend to my help, O LORD of my salvation.

God, make speed to save us. LORD, make haste to help us.

Make haste, O LORD, to deliver us from all our sins, who reigns with you and the Holy Spirit, now and ever, and unto the ages of ages. Amen.

Protect us, O LORD, as the pupil of your eye, protect us under the shadow of your wings.

Deign to protect and sanctify us all, Almighty God, who reigns with you and the Holy Spirit, now and ever, and unto the ages of ages. Amen.

Symbol of Faith

We believe in God, the Father almighty, unseen, creator of creatures seen and unseen. We believe in Jesus Christ, His only Son, our LORD, almighty God, conceived by the power of the Holy Spirit, born from the Virgin Mary, suffered under Pontius Pilate; who was crucified, died, and was buried; He descended into Hell; on the third day he rose again from the dead; He ascended into heaven, and is seated at the right hand of God the Father Almighty; from there He will come to judge the living and the dead. We believe in the Holy Spirit, almighty God, of one substance with the Father and Son. The holy catholic church, the forgiveness of sins, communion of saints, and the resurrection of the dead. We believe in life after death, and eternal life in the glory of Christ. All these things we believe in God. Amen.

Divine Prayer

As taught by divine instruction and guided by divine institution, we dare to say:

Our Father in heaven, hallowed be your name; your kingdom come, your will be done, on earth as it is in heaven. Give us today our substantial bread. Forgive us our debts as we forgive our debtors. Keep us from falling into temptation and deliver us from evil. Amen.

For yours is the kingdom, and the power, and the glory of the Father, and the Son, and Holy Spirit, now and ever, and unto the ages of ages. Amen.

The Order of Sext

Invitatory

God, make speed to save us. LORD, make haste to help us.

Glory to the Father, and to the Son, and to the Holy Spirit, now and ever, and unto the ages of ages. Amen.

Hasten, O LORD, to free us from all our sins; for you live and reign with the eternal living Father and the Holy Spirit, now and ever, and unto the ages of ages. Amen.

We have sinned, O LORD, we have sinned, spare us our sins, and save us; you who guided Noah over the flood waves, hear us; who with your word recalled Jonah from the abyss; deliver us; who stretched forth your hand to Peter as he sank, help us, O Christ. Son of God, you accomplished marvelous things of the LORD with our fathers, be favorable in our days also; Stretch forth your hand from on high.

Deliver us, O Christ. Hear us, O Christ. Hear us, O Christ. Hear us, O Lord have mercy.

Son of God, you who did marvelous things of the LORD with our fathers, be favorable in our days also; Stretch forth your hand from on high. Deliver us, O Christ. Hear us, O Christ.

A Collect for the Hour of Sext

Spare your suppliant
As they pray at the sixth hour
Where you were for all
O Christ, placed on the cross,

Who reigns now and ever,

And unto the ages of ages. Amen.

Another

Almighty eternal God, who has done great things for us, at the sixth hour you ascended to the Holy Cross and enlightened the darkness of the world. Deign to enlighten our hearts, who reigns with the Father and the Holy Spirit, now and ever, and unto the ages of ages. Amen.

66

Deus misereatur

May God have mercy on us, and bless us: may he cause the light of his countenance to shine upon us, and may he have mercy on us. That we may know thy way upon earth: thy salvation in all nations. Let people confess to thee, O God: let all people give praise to thee. Let the nations be glad and rejoice: for thou judgest the people with justice, and directest the nations upon earth. Let the people, O God, confess to thee: let all the people give praise to thee: The earth hath yielded her fruit. May God, our God bless us, May God bless us: and all the ends of the earth fear him.

69

Deus, in adjutorium

O God, come to my assistance; O LORD, make haste to help me. Let them be confounded and ashamed that seek my soul: Let them be turned backward, and blush for shame that desire evils to me: Let them be presently turned away blushing for shame that say to me: Tis well, tis well. Let all that seek thee rejoice and be glad in thee; and let such as love thy salvation say always: The LORD be magnified. But I am needy and poor; O God, help me. Thou art my helper and my deliverer: O LORD, make no delay.

115

Credidi, propter quod

I have believed, therefore have I spoken; but I have been humbled exceedingly. I said in my excess: Every man is a liar. What shall I render to the
LORD, for all the things he hath rendered unto me? I will take the chalice
of salvation; and I will call upon the name of the LORD. I will pay my vows
to the LORD before all his people: Precious in the sight of the Lord is the
death of his saints. O LORD, for I am thy servant: I am thy servant, and the
son of thy handmaid. Thou hast broken my bonds: I will sacrifice to thee
the sacrifice of praise, and I will call upon the name of the LORD. I will pay
my vows to the Lord in the sight of all his people: In the courts of the house
of the LORD, in the midst of thee, O Jerusalem.

God, make speed to save us. Lord, make haste to help us.

Glory to the Father, and to the Son, and to the Holy Spirit, now and ever,
and unto the ages of ages. Amen.

A Collect for After the Psalms

Most High God, king of the angels,

God, praise of all elements,

God, glory and joy of the saints,

Guard the souls of your servants,

Who reigns now and ever,

And unto the ages of ages. Amen.

Hymn

Here may be sung a canticle or hymn.

A Collect for After the Hymn

Look down, O Lord, at our prayers, you who visits feeble humans, and bestow on us your sanctification and immortality, O Christ, who reigns with

122

the Father and the Holy Spirit, now and ever, and unto the ages of ages. Amen.

Gospel

The Gospel According to St. Mark

MARK 15:33–41

When the sixth hour had come, there was darkness over the whole earth until the ninth hour. At the ninth hour Jesus cried out with a loud voice, "Eloi, Eloi, lema sabachthani?" which means, "My God, my God, why have you forsaken me?" When some of the standers heard it, they said, "Behold, he is calling for Elijah." And one ran, filling a sponge with sour wine, put it on a stick, and gave him a drink, saying, "Stay, let us see if Elijah will come to take him down." Then Jesus cried out with a loud voice and gave up the ghost. And the veil of the temple was torn in two, from the top to the bottom. And the centurion who stood facing, seeing the way he had given up the ghost, he said, "Indeed this man was the son of God!"

Amen, thanks be to God.

A Collect for After the Gospel

May the spiritual songs and delightful hymns we sing to you, O Christ, please your majesty, as we offer our spiritual sacrifice; who lives and reigns with the eternal living Father and the Holy Spirit, now and ever, and unto the ages of ages. Amen.

Common Prayer

I put my trust in you, O LORD; let me never be confounded. Deliver me in your justice and rescue me.

O LORD my God, do not depart from me; Attend to my help, O LORD of my salvation.

God, make speed to save us. LORD, make haste to help us.

Make haste, O LORD, to deliver us from all our sins, who reigns with the Father and the Holy Spirit, now and ever, and unto the ages of ages. Amen.

Protect us, O LORD, as the pupil of your eye, protect us under the shadow of your wings.

Deign to protect and sanctify us all, Almighty God, who reigns with the Father and the Holy Spirit, now and ever, and unto the ages of ages. Amen.

Symbol of Faith

We believe in God, the Father almighty, unseen, creator of creatures seen and unseen. We believe in Jesus Christ, His only Son, our LORD, almighty God, conceived by the power of the Holy Spirit, born from the Virgin Mary, suffered under Pontius Pilate; who was crucified, died, and was buried; He descended into Hell; on the third day he rose again from the dead; He ascended into heaven, and is seated at the right hand of God the Father Almighty; from there He will come to judge the living and the dead. We believe in the Holy Spirit, almighty God, of one substance with the Father and Son. The holy catholic church, the forgiveness of sins, communion of saints, and the resurrection of the dead. We believe in life after death, and eternal life in the glory of Christ. All these things we believe in God. Amen.

Divine Prayer

As taught by divine instruction and guided by divine institution, we dare to say:

Our Father in heaven, hallowed be your name; your kingdom come, your will be done, on earth as it is in heaven. Give us today our substantial bread. Forgive us our debts as we forgive our debtors. Keep us from falling into temptation and deliver us from evil. Amen.

For yours is the kingdom, and the power, and the glory of the Father, and the Son, and Holy Spirit, now and ever, and unto the ages of ages. Amen.

The Order of None

Invitatory

God, make speed to save us. LORD, make haste to help us.

Glory to the Father, and to the Son, and to the Holy Spirit, now and ever, and unto the ages of ages. Amen.

Hasten, O LORD, to free us from all our sins; for you live and reign with the eternal living Father and the Holy Spirit, now and ever, and unto the ages of ages. Amen.

We have sinned, O LORD, we have sinned, spare us our sins, and save us; you who guided Noah over the flood waves, hear us; who with your word recalled Jonah from the abyss; deliver us; who stretched forth your hand to Peter as he sank, help us, O Christ. Son of God, you accomplished marvelous things of the LORD with our fathers, be favorable in our days also; Stretch forth your hand from on high.

Deliver us, O Christ. Hear us, O Christ. Hear us, O Christ. Hear us, O Lord have mercy.

Son of God, you who did marvelous things of the LORD with our fathers, be favorable in our days also; Stretch forth your hand from on high. Deliver us, O Christ. Hear us, O Christ.

A Collect for the Hour of None

Hear the prayers of all
At the ninth hour,
When, O Christ, Cornelius
Was visited by an angel,

Who reigns now and ever,

and unto the ages of ages. Amen.

Another

It is the ninth hour of the day to you, O LORD, by direct supplication, show your divine miracles to your worshipers, enlightening our hearts by imitation, who reigns with you and the Holy Spirit, now and ever, and unto the ages of ages. Amen.

Another

Come together, most beloved brothers, to the ninth prayer, the time at which the robber confessed and was promised the kingdom of heaven, so do we. O LORD, we confess our sins, that we may obtain the kingdom of heaven and merit eternal life, who reigns with you and the Holy Spirit, now and ever, and unto the ages of ages. Amen.

129

De profundis

Out of the depths I have cried to thee, O LORD: LORD, hear my voice. Let thy ears be attentive to the voice of my supplication. If thou, O LORD, wilt mark iniquities: Lord, who shall stand it. For with thee there is merciful forgiveness: and by reason of thy law, I have waited for thee, O LORD. My soul hath relied on his word: My soul hath hoped in the LORD. From the morning watch even until night, let Israel hope in the LORD. Because with the LORD there is mercy: and with him plentiful redemption. And he shall redeem Israel from all his iniquities.

132

Ecce, quam bonum!

Behold how good and how pleasant it is for brethren to dwell in unity. Like the precious ointment on the head, that ran down upon the beard, the beard of Aaron, Which ran down to the skirt of his garment: As the dew of Hermon, which descendeth upon mount Sion. For there the LORD hath commandeth blessing, and life forevermore.

147

Lauda Jerusalem Dominum

Praise the LORD, O Jerusalem: praise thy God, O Zion. Because he hath strengthened the bolts of thy gates, he hath blessed thy children within thee. Who hath placed peace in thy borders: and filleth thee with the fat of corn. Who sendeth forth his speech to the earth: his word runneth swiftly. Who giveth snow like wool: scattereth mists like ashes. He sendeth his crystal like morsels: who shall stand before the face of his cold? He shall send out his word, and shall melt them: his wind shall blow, and the waters shall run. Who declareth his word to Jacob: his justices and his judgments to Israel. He hath not done in like manner to every nation: and his judgments he hath not made manifest to them. Alleluia.

God, make speed to save us. Lord, make haste to help us.

Glory to the Father, and to the Son, and to the Holy Spirit, now and ever, and unto the ages of ages. Amen.

A Collect for after the Psalms

Most High God, king of the angels,
God, praise of all elements,
God, glory and joy of the saints,
Guard the souls of your servants,
Who reigns now and ever,
and unto the ages of ages. Amen.

Hymn

Here may be sung a canticle or hymn.

A Collect for After the Hymn

Look down, O LORD, at our prayers, you who visits feeble humans, and bestow on us your sanctification and immortality, O Christ, who reigns with the Father and the Holy Spirit, now and ever, and unto the ages of ages. Amen.

Gospel

The Gospel According to Acts

ACTS 10:30–36

Cornelius replied, "Four days ago at this hour, I was praying in my house at the ninth hour when a man stood before me in white apparel. He said, 'Cornelius, your prayer is heard and your alms have been remembered in the sight of God. Send therefore to Joppa and ask for Simon, who is called Peter; he is staying in the house of Simon, a tanner, by the sea.' Therefore I sent to you and you have done well in coming. Therefore we are all present in your sight, to hear all things are commanded to you by the Lord." Then Peter opened his mouth, saying, "I truly understand that God shows no partiality, but in every nation who fears him and does what is right and is acceptable to him. God sent the word to the children of Israel, preaching peace by Jesus Christ for he is Lord of all.

Amen, thanks be to God.

A Collect for After the Gospel

May the spiritual songs and delightful hymns we sing to you, O Christ, please your majesty, as we offer our spiritual sacrifice; who lives and reigns with the eternal living Father and the Holy Spirit, now and ever, and unto the ages of ages. Amen.

Common Prayer

I put my trust in you, O LORD; let me never be confounded. Deliver me in your justice and rescue me.

O LORD my God, do not depart from me; Attend to my help, O LORD of my salvation.

God, make speed to save us. LORD, make haste to help us.

Make haste, O LORD, to deliver us from all our sins, who reigns with the Father and the Holy Spirit, now and ever, and unto the ages of ages. Amen.

Protect us, O LORD, as the pupil of your eye, protect us under the shadow of your wings.

Deign to protect and sanctify us all, Almighty God, who reigns with the Father and the Holy Spirit, now and ever, and unto the ages of ages. Amen.

Symbol of Faith

We believe in God, the Father almighty, unseen, creator of creatures seen and unseen. We believe in Jesus Christ, His only Son, our LORD, almighty God, conceived by the power of the Holy Spirit, born from the Virgin Mary, suffered under Pontius Pilate; who was crucified, died, and was buried; He descended into Hell; on the third day he rose again from the dead; He ascended into heaven, and is seated at the right hand of God the Father Almighty; from there He will come to judge the living and the dead. We believe in the Holy Spirit, almighty God, of one substance with the Father and Son. The holy catholic church, the forgiveness of sins, communion of saints, and the resurrection of the dead. We believe in life after death, and eternal life in the glory of Christ. All these things we believe in God. Amen.

Divine Prayer

As taught by divine instruction and guided by divine institution, we dare to say:

Our Father in heaven, hallowed be your name; your kingdom come, your will be done, on earth as it is in heaven. Give us today our substantial bread. Forgive us our debts as we forgive our debtors. Keep us from falling into temptation and deliver us from evil. Amen.

For yours is the kingdom, and the power, and the glory of the Father, and the Son, and Holy Spirit, now and ever, and unto the ages of ages. Amen.

The Order of Vespers

Invitatory

God, make speed to save us. LORD, make haste to help us.

Glory to the Father, and to the Son, and to the Holy Spirit, now and ever, and unto the ages of ages. Amen.

Hasten, O LORD, to free us from all our sins; for you live and reign with the eternal living Father and the Holy Spirit, now and ever, and unto the ages of ages. Amen.

We have sinned, O LORD, we have sinned, spare us our sins, and save us; you who guided Noah over the flood waves, hear us; who with your word recalled Jonah from the abyss; deliver us; who stretched forth your hand to Peter as he sank, help us, O Christ. Son of God, you accomplished marvelous things of the LORD with our fathers, be favorable in our days also; Stretch forth your hand from on high.

Deliver us, O Christ. Hear us, O Christ. Hear us, O Christ. Hear us, O LORD have mercy.

Son of God, you who did marvelous things of the LORD with our fathers, be favorable in our days also; Stretch forth your hand from on high. Deliver us, O Christ. Hear us, O Christ.

A Collect for after the Hour of Vespers

In the evening hours,
We call upon you, O LORD
To receive our yearly prayers
And to forgive our sins

Who reigns now and ever,

And unto the ages of ages. Amen.

Another

In the evening hour, let our prayers ascend to the ears of your divine majesty. Let your blessing descend upon us, O LORD, as we have hoped in you, who reigns with the Father and the Holy Spirit, now and ever, and unto the ages of ages. Amen.

64

Te decet hymnus

A Hymn, O God, becometh thee in Zion: and a vow shall be paid to thee in Jerusalem. O hear my prayer: all flesh shall come to thee. The words of the wicked have prevailed over us: and thou wilt pardon our transgressions. Blessed is he whom thou hast chosen and taken to thee: he shall dwell in thy courts. We shall be filled with the good things of thy house; holy is thy temple, Wonderful in justice. Hear us, O God our saviour, who art the hope of all the ends of the earth, and in the sea afar off. Thou who preparest the mountains by thy strength, being girded with power: Who troublest the depth of the sea, the noise of its waves. The Gentiles shall be troubled, And they that dwell in the uttermost borders shall be afraid at thy signs: thou shalt make the outgoings of the morning and of the evening to be joyful. Thou hast visited the earth, and hast plentifully watered it; thou hast many ways enriched it. The river of God is filled with water, thou hast prepared their food: for so is its preparation. Fill up plentifully the streams thereof, multiply its fruits; it shall spring up and rejoice in its showers. Thou shalt bless the crown of the year of thy goodness: and thy fields shall be filled with plenty. The beautiful places of the wilderness shall grow fat: and the hills shall be girded about with joy, The rams of the flock are clothed, and the vales shall abound with corn: they shall shout, yea they shall sing a hymn.

103

Benedic, anima mea

Bless the LORD, O my soul: O LORD my God, thou art exceedingly great. Thou hast put on praise and beauty: And art clothed with light as with a garment. Who stretchest out the heaven like a pavilion: Who coverest the higher rooms thereof with water. Who makest the clouds thy chariot: who walkest upon the wings of the winds. Who makest thy angels spirits: and thy ministers a burning fire. Who hast founded the earth upon its own bases: it shall not be moved forever and ever. The deep like a garment is its clothing: above the mountains shall the waters stand. At thy rebuke they shall flee: at the voice of thy thunder they shall fear. The mountains ascend, and the plains descend into the place which thou hast founded for them. Thou hast set a bound which they shall not pass over; neither shall they return to cover the earth. Thou sendest forth springs in the vales: between the midst of the hills the waters shall pass. All the beasts of the field shall drink: the wild asses shall expect in their thirst. Over them the birds of the air shall dwell: from the midst of the rocks they shall give forth their voices. Thou waterest the hills from thy upper rooms: the earth shall be filled with the fruit of thy works: Bringing forth grass for cattle, and herb for the service of men. That thou mayst bring bread out of the earth: And that wine may cheer the heart of man. That he may make the face cheerful with oil: and that bread may strengthen man's heart. The trees of the field shall be filled, and the cedars of Libanus which he hath planted: There the sparrows shall make their nests. The highest of them is the house of the heron. The high hills are a refuge for the harts, the rock for the irchins. He hath made the moon for seasons: the sun knoweth his going down. Thou hast appointed darkness, and it is night: in it shall all the beasts of the woods go about: The young lions roaring after their prey, and seeking their meat from God. The sun ariseth, and they are gathered together: and they shall lie down in their dens. Man shall go forth to his work, and to his labour until the evening. How great are thy works, O LORD? thou hast made all things in wisdom: the earth is filled with thy riches. So is this great sea, which stretcheth wide its arms: there are creeping things without number: Creatures little and great. There the ships shall go. This sea dragon which thou hast formed to play therein. All expect of thee that thou give them food in season. What thou givest to them they shall gather up: when thou openest thy hand, they shall all be filled with good. But if thou turnest away thy face, they shall be troubled: thou shalt take away their breath, and they shall fail, and shall return to their dust. Thou shalt send forth thy spirit, and they shall be created: and thou shalt renew the face of the earth. May the glory of the LORD endure for ever: the LORD shall rejoice in his works. He looketh upon the earth, and maketh it tremble: he toucheth the mountains, and they smoke. I will sing to the LORD as long as I live: I will sing praise to my God while I have my being. Let my speech be acceptable to him: but I will take delight in the LORD. Let sinners be consumed out of the earth, and the unjust, so that they be no more: O my soul, bless thou the LORD.

112

Laudate, pueri

Praise the LORD, ye children: praise ye the name of the LORD. Blessed be the name of the LORD, from henceforth now and forever. From the rising of the sun unto the going down of the same, the name of the LORD is worthy of praise. The LORD is high above all nations; and his glory above the heavens. Who is as the LORD our God, who dwelleth on high: And looketh down on the low things in heaven and in earth? Raising up the needy from the earth, and lifting up the poor out of the dunghill: That he may place him with princes, with the princes of his people. Who maketh a barren woman to dwell in a house, the joyful mother of children.

119

Ad Dominum

In my trouble I cried to the LORD: and he heard me. O LORD, deliver my soul from wicked lips, and a deceitful tongue. What shall be given to thee, or what shall be added to thee, to a deceitful tongue? The sharp arrows of the mighty, with coals that lay waste. Woe is me, that my sojourning is prolonged! I have dwelt with the inhabitants of cedar: My soul hath been long a sojourner. With them that hated peace I was peaceable: when I spoke to them they fought against me without cause.

120

Levavi oculos

I have lifted up my eyes to the mountains, from whence help shall come to me. My help is from the LORD, who made heaven and earth. May he not suffer thy foot to be moved: neither let him slumber that keepeth thee. Behold he shall neither slumber nor sleep, that keepeth Israel. The LORD is thy keeper, the LORD is thy protection upon thy right hand. The sun shall not burn thee by day: nor the moon by night. The LORD keepeth thee from all evil: may the LORD keep thy soul. May the LORD keep thy coming in and thy going out; from henceforth now and forever.

121

Laetatus sum

I rejoiced at the things that were said to me: We shall go into the house of the LORD. Our feet were standing in thy courts, O Jerusalem. Jerusalem, which is built as a city, which is compact together. For thither did the tribes go up, the tribes of the LORD: the testimony of Israel, to praise the name of the LORD. Because their seats have sat in judgment, seats upon the house of David. Pray ye for the things that are for the peace of Jerusalem: and abundance for them that love thee. Let peace be in thy strength: and abundance in thy towers. For the sake of my brethren, and of my neighbours, I spoke peace of thee. Because of the house of the LORD our God, I have sought good things for thee.

122

Ad te levavi oculos meos

To thee have I lifted up my eyes, who dwellest in heaven. Behold as the eyes of the servants are on the hands of their masters, As the eyes of the hand-maid are on the hands of her mistress: so are our eyes unto the LORD our God, until he have mercy on us. Have mercy on us, O LORD, have mercy on us: for we are greatly filled with contempt. For our soul is greatly filled: we are a reproach to the rich, and contempt to the proud.

123

Nisi quia Dominus

If it had not been that the LORD was with us, let Israel now say: If it had not been that the LORD was with us, When men rose up against us, Perhaps they had swallowed us up alive. When their fury was enkindled against us, Perhaps the waters had swallowed us up. Our soul hath passed through a torrent: perhaps our soul had passed through a water insupportable. Blessed be the LORD, who hath not given us to be a prey to their teeth. Our soul hath been delivered as a sparrow out of the snare of the fowlers. The snare is broken, and we are delivered. Our help is in the name of the LORD, who made heaven and earth.

124

Qui confidunt

They that trust in the LORD shall be as mount Zion: he shall not be moved forever that dwelleth In Jerusalem. Mountains are round about it: so the LORD is round about his people from henceforth now and forever. For the LORD will not leave the rod of sinners upon the lot of the just: that the just may not stretch forth their hands to iniquity. Do good, O LORD, to those that are good, and to the upright of heart. But such as turn aside into bonds, the LORD shall lead out with the workers of iniquity: peace upon Israel.

125

In convertendo

When the LORD brought back the captivity of Zion, we became like men comforted. Then was our mouth filled with gladness; and our tongue with joy. Then shall they say among the Gentiles: The LORD hath done great things for them. The LORD hath done great things for us: we are become joyful. Turn again our captivity, O LORD, as a stream in the south. They that sow in tears shall reap in joy. Going they went and wept, casting their seeds. But coming they shall come with joyfulness, carrying their sheaves.

126

Nisi Dominus

Unless the LORD build the house, they labour in vain that build it. Unless the LORD keep the city, he watcheth in vain that keepeth it. It is vain for you to rise before light, rise ye after you have sitten, you that eat the bread of sorrow. When he shall give sleep to his beloved, Behold the inheritance of the LORD are children: the reward, the fruit of the womb. As arrows in the hand of the mighty, so the children of them that have been shaken. Blessed is the man that hath filled the desire with them; he shall not be confounded when he shall speak to his enemies in the gate.

127

Beati omnes

Blessed are all they that fear the LORD: that walk in his ways. For thou shalt eat the labours of thy hands: blessed art thou, and it shall be well with thee. Thy wife as a fruitful vine, on the sides of thy house. Behold, thus shall the man be blessed that feareth the LORD. May the LORD bless thee out of Zion: and mayest thou see the good things of Jerusalem all the days of thy life. And mayest thou see thy children's children, peace upon Israel.

128

Saepe expugnaverunt

Often have they fought against me from my youth, let Israel now say. Often have they fought against me from my youth: but they could not prevail over me. The wicked have wrought upon my back: they have lengthened their iniquity. The LORD who is just will cut the necks of sinners: Let them all be confounded and turned back that hate Zion. Let them be as grass on the tops of houses: which withered before it be plucked up: Wherewith the mower fills not his hand: nor he that gathers sheaves his bosom. And they that have passed by have not said: The blessing of the LORD be upon you: we have blessed you in the name of the LORD.

129

De profundis

Out of the depths I have cried to you, O LORD: LORD, hear my voice. Let your ears be attentive to the voice of my supplication. If thou, O LORD, will mark iniquities: LORD, who shall stand it. For with you there is merciful forgiveness: and by reason of your law, I have waited for you, O LORD. My soul has relied on his word: My soul has hoped in the LORD. From the morning watch even until night, let Israel hope in the LORD. Because with the LORD there is mercy: and with him plentiful redemption. And he shall redeem Israel from all his iniquities.

130

Domine non, est.

LORD, my heart is not exalted: nor are my eyes lofty. Neither have I walked in great matters, nor in wonderful things above me. If I was not humbly minded but exalted my soul: As a child that is weaned is towards his mother, so reward in my soul. Let Israel hope in the LORD, from henceforth now and forever.

131

Memento, Domine

O LORD, remember David, and all his meekness. How he swore to the LORD, he vowed a vow to the God of Jacob: If I shall enter into the tabernacle of my house: if I shall go up into the bed wherein I lie: If I shall give sleep to my eyes, or slumber to my eyelids, Or rest to my temples: until I find out a place for the LORD, a tabernacle for the God of Jacob. Behold we have heard of it in Ephrata: we have found it in the fields of the wood. We will go into his tabernacle: We will adore in the place where his feet stood. Arise, O LORD, into thy resting place: thou and the ark, which thou hast sanctified. Let thy priests be clothed with justice: and let thy saints rejoice. For thy servant David's sake, turn not away the face of thy anointed. The LORD hath sworn truth to David, and he will not make it void: of the fruit of thy womb I will set upon thy throne. If thy children will keep thy covenant, and these my testimonies which I shall teach them: Their children also for evermore shall sit upon thy throne. For the LORD hath chosen Zion: he hath chosen it for his dwelling. This is my rest for ever and ever: here will I dwell, for I have chosen it. Blessing, I will bless her widow: I will satisfy her poor with bread. I will clothe her priests with salvation: and her saints shall rejoice with exceeding great joy. There will I bring forth a horn to David: I have prepared a lamp for my anointed. His enemies I will clothe with confusion: but upon him will my sanctification flourish.

132

Ecce, quam bonum!

Behold how good and how pleasant it is for brethren to dwell in unity. Like the precious ointment on the head, that ran down upon the beard, the beard of Aaron, Which ran down to the skirt of his garment: As the dew of Hermon, which descends upon mount Sion. For there the LORD has commanded blessing, and life for evermore.

133

Ecce nunc benedicite

Behold now bless the LORD, all you servants of the LORD: Who stand in the house of the LORD, in the courts of the house of our God. In the nights lift up your hands to the holy places and bless the LORD. May the LORD out of Zion bless you, he that made heaven and earth.

God, make speed to save us. LORD, make haste to help us.

Glory to the Father, and to the Son, and to the Holy Spirit, now and ever, and unto the ages of ages. Amen.

A Collect for after the Psalms

God, to whom the heavenly hosts sing,
To whom the saintly church praise,
To whom all spirits worship in song,

Have mercy on all your people,

Who reigns now and ever,

and unto the ages of ages. Amen.

Hymn

Glory Be to God

Gloria in Excelsis Deo

FROM BOOK OF COMMON PRAYER, 1662

Glory be to God on high

And in earth peace, goodwill towards men,

We praise thee, we bless thee,

we worship thee, we glorify thee,

we give thanks to thee, for thy great glory

O LORD God, heavenly King,

God the Father Almighty.

O LORD, the only-begotten Son, Jesu Christ;

O LORD God, Lamb of God, Son of the Father,

that takest away the sins of the world,

have mercy upon us.

Thou that takest away the sins of the world,

have mercy upon us.

Thou that takest away the sins of the world,

receive our prayer.

Thou that sittest at the right hand of God the Father,

have mercy upon us.

For thou only art holy;

thou only art the LORD;

thou only, O Christ,

with the Holy Ghost,

art most high

in the glory of God the Father.

Amen.

A Collect for after the Hymn

Look down, O LORD, at our prayers, You who visits feeble humans, and bestow on us your sanctification and immortality, O Christ, who reigns with the eternal living Father and the Holy Spirit, now and ever, and unto the ages of ages. Amen.

Gospel

The Gospel According to St. Luke

LUKE 4:38–41

And after Jesus left the synagogue, he went into Simon's house. Simon's mother-in-law was suffering with a great fever, and they besought him for her. Then he stood over her and rebuked the fever, and it left her. Immediately rising, she ministered to them. As the sun was setting, all those who were sick with diverse diseases brought them to him; and he laid his hands on every one of them, healed them. And devils went out from many, crying out and saying, "You are the Son of God!" But he rebuked them and suffered them not to speak, for they knew that he was Christ.

Amen, thanks be to God.

A Collect for after the Gospel

May the spiritual songs and delightful hymns we sing to you, O Christ, please your majesty, as we offer our spiritual sacrifice; who lives and reigns with the eternal living Father and the Holy Spirit, now and ever, and unto the ages of ages. Amen.

Common Prayer

Remember not the iniquities of our bygone ways and let your mercy come before us quickly, for we have become exceeding poor.

Help us, O God our Savior, for the glory of your name. LORD, deliver us and forgive our sins for your name's sake. Do not give up to the beasts the soul that confesses to you. Forget not the souls of your poor forever. Look upon your covenant, O LORD, who reigns now and ever, and unto the ages of ages. Amen.

For our sins

O God, come to my aid. O LORD, make haste to help me.

Make haste, O LORD, to deliver us from all our sins, who reigns now and ever, and unto the ages of ages. Amen.

For those to be baptized

Save your people, O LORD, and bless your heritage. Rule them and lift them up forever.

Have mercy, O LORD, on your catholic church, which you have redeemed in your holy blood, who reigns now and ever, and unto the ages of ages. Amen.

For the clergy

Arise, O LORD, and go into your eternal peace, you and the ark of your holiness. Your priests will be clothed with justice and your saints exalted.

Let all your saints rejoice in you, O LORD, who places their hope in you in all truth, now and ever, and unto the ages of ages. Amen.

For the people and their leaders

The LORD will give strength to His people; The LORD bless His people in peace.

For the martyrs

By the virtue of your eternal name, Almighty God, we pray you to make us companions of martyrs and of all your saints by the merits of your saints, equal in faith, vigorous in devotion, and like in passion, to make us equal in the resurrection of the fortunate, who reigns now and ever, and unto the ages of ages. Amen.

For the penitents

Have mercy on me, O God, your second great mercy.

Grant us, O LORD, pardon to those who ask you out of faith your second great mercy, O God, who reigns now and ever, and unto the ages of ages. Amen.

Symbol of Faith

We believe in God, the Father almighty, unseen, creator of creatures seen and unseen. We believe in Jesus Christ, His only Son, our LORD, almighty God, conceived by the power of the Holy Spirit, born from the Virgin Mary, suffered under Pontius Pilate; who was crucified, died, and was buried; He descended into Hell; on the third day he rose again from the dead; He ascended into heaven, and is seated at the right hand of God the Father Almighty; from there He will come to judge the living and the dead. We believe in the Holy Spirit, almighty God, of one substance with the Father and Son. The holy catholic church, the forgiveness of sins, communion of saints, and the resurrection of the dead. We believe in life after death, and eternal life in the glory of Christ. All these things we believe in God. Amen.

Divine Prayer

As taught by divine instruction and guided by divine institution, we dare to say:

Our Father in heaven, hallowed be your name; your kingdom come, your will be done, on earth as it is in heaven. Give us today our substantial bread.

Forgive us our debts as we forgive our debtors. Keep us from falling into temptation and deliver us from evil. Amen.

For yours is the kingdom, and the power, and the glory of the Father, and the Son, and Holy Spirit, now and ever, and unto the ages of ages. Amen.

The Order of Duodecima

Invitatory

God, make speed to save us. LORD, make haste to help us.

Glory to the Father, and to the Son, and to the Holy Spirit, now and ever, and unto the ages of ages. Amen.

Hasten, O LORD, to free us from all our sins; for you live and reign with the eternal living Father and the Holy Spirit, now and ever, and unto the ages of ages. Amen.

We have sinned, O LORD, we have sinned, spare us our sins, and save us; you who guided Noah over the flood waves, hear us; who with your word recalled Jonah from the abyss; deliver us; who stretched forth your hand to Peter as he sank, help us, O Christ. Son of God, you accomplished marvelous things of the LORD with our fathers, be favorable in our days also; Stretch forth your hand from on high.

Deliver us, O Christ. Hear us, O Christ. Hear us, O Christ. Hear us, O LORD have mercy.

Son of God, you who did marvelous things of the LORD with our fathers, be favorable in our days also; Stretch forth your hand from on high. Deliver us, O Christ. Hear us, O Christ.

A Collect for the Hour of Duodecima

O God, who illuminates the inescapable darkness of the night, illuminating the dense darkness, we beseech you, O LORD, to keep our heart in the work of your commandments, who lives and reigns with the eternal living Father and the Holy Spirit, now and ever, and unto the ages of ages. Amen.

Another

Now as the time of day unfolds and the time of night passes over, let us beseech the mercy of God that we, being supplied with divine senses, may renounce the works of darkness, who lives and reigns forever and ever. Amen.

Another

As we endure the time of night

O Christ, we praise;

Have mercy on us

Praying for you from our heart

Who lives and reigns now and ever,

And unto the ages of ages. Amen.

128

Saepe expugnaverunt

Often have they fought against me from my youth, let Israel now say. Often have they fought against me from my youth: but they could not prevail over me. The wicked have wrought upon my back: they have lengthened their iniquity. The LORD who is just will cut the necks of sinners: Let them all be confounded and turned back that hate Zion. Let them be as grass on the tops of houses: which withered before it be plucked up: Wherewith the mower filleth not his hand: nor he that gathereth sheaves his bosom. And they that have passed by have not said: The blessing of the LORD be upon you: we have blessed you in the name of the LORD.

129

De profundis

Out of the depths I have cried to thee, O LORD: LORD, hear my voice. Let thy ears be attentive to the voice of my supplication. If thou, O LORD, wilt mark iniquities: LORD, who shall stand it. For with thee there is merciful forgiveness: and by reason of thy law, I have waited for thee, O LORD. My soul hath relied on his word: My soul hath hoped in the LORD. From the morning watch even until night, let Israel hope in the LORD. Because with the LORD there is mercy: and with him plentiful redemption. And he shall redeem Israel from all his iniquities.

130

Domine, non est

LORD, my heart is not exalted: nor are my eyes lofty. Neither have I walked in great matters, nor in wonderful things above me. If I was not humbly minded, but exalted my soul: As a child that is weaned is towards his mother, so reward in my soul. Let Israel hope in the LORD, from henceforth now and forever.

131

Memento, Domine

O LORD, remember David, and all his meekness. How he swore to the LORD, he vowed a vow to the God of Jacob: If I shall enter into the tabernacle of my house: if I shall go up into the bed wherein I lie: If I shall give sleep to my eyes, or slumber to my eyelids, Or rest to my temples: until I find out a place for the LORD, a tabernacle for the God of Jacob. Behold we have heard of it in Ephrata: we have found it in the fields of the wood. We will go into his tabernacle: We will adore in the place where his feet stood. Arise, O LORD, into thy resting place: thou and the ark, which thou hast sanctified. Let thy priests be clothed with justice: and let thy saints rejoice. For thy servant David's sake, turn not away the face of thy anointed. The LORD hath sworn truth to David, and he will not make it void: of the fruit of thy womb I will set upon thy throne. If thy children will keep thy covenant, and these my testimonies which I shall teach them: Their children also for evermore shall sit upon thy throne. For the LORD hath chosen Zion: he hath chosen it for his dwelling. This is my rest for ever and ever: here will I dwell, for I have chosen it. Blessing, I will bless her widow: I will satisfy her poor with bread. I will clothe her priests with salvation: and her saints shall rejoice with exceeding great joy. There will I bring forth a horn to David: I have prepared a lamp for my anointed. His enemies I will clothe with confusion: but upon him will my sanctification flourish.

132

Ecce, quam bonum

Behold how good and how pleasant it is for brethren to dwell in unity. Like the precious ointment on the head, that ran down upon the beard, the beard of Aaron, Which ran down to the skirt of his garment: As the dew of Hermon, which descendeth upon mount Zion. For there the LORD hath commandeth blessing, and life forevermore.

134

Laudate nomen

Praise ye the name of the LORD: O you his servants, praise the LORD: You that stand in the house of the LORD, in the courts of the house of our God. Praise ye the LORD, for the LORD is good: sing ye to his name, for it is sweet. For the LORD hath chosen Jacob unto himself: Israel for his own possession. For I have known that the LORD is great, and our God is above all gods. Whatsoever the LORD hath pleased he hath done, in heaven, in earth, in the sea, and in all the deeps. He bringeth up clouds from the end of the earth: he hath made lightnings for the rain. He bringeth forth winds out of his stores: He slew the firstborn of Egypt from man even unto beast. He sent forth signs and wonders in the midst of thee, O Egypt: upon Pharaoh, and upon all his servants. He smote many nations, and slew mighty kings: Sehon king of the Amorrhites, and Og king of Basan, and all the kingdoms of Chanaan. And gave their land for an inheritance, for an inheritance to his people Israel. Thy name, O LORD, is forever: thy memorial, O LORD, unto all generations. For the LORD will judge his people, and will be entreated in favour of his servants. The idols of the Gentiles are silver and gold, the works of men's hands. They have a mouth, but they speak not: they have eyes, but they see not. They have ears, but they hear not: neither is there any breath in their mouths. Let them that make them be like to them: and everyone that trusteth in them. Bless the LORD, O house of Israel: bless the LORD, O house of Aaron. Bless the

LORD, O house of Levi: you that fear the LORD, bless the LORD. Blessed be the LORD out of Zion, who dwelleth in Jerusalem.

136

Super flumina

Upon the rivers of Babylon, there we sat and wept: when we remembered Zion: On the willows in the midst thereof we hung up our instruments. For there they that led us into captivity required of us the words of songs. And they that carried us away, said: Sing ye to us a hymn of the songs of Zion. How shall we sing the song of the LORD in a strange land? If I forget thee, O Jerusalem, let my right hand be forgotten. Let my tongue cleave to my jaws, if I do not remember thee: If I make not Jerusalem the beginning of my joy. Remember, O LORD, the children of Edom, in the day of Jerusalem: Who say: Rase it, rase it, even to the foundation thereof. O daughter of Babylon, miserable: blessed shall he be who shall repay thee thy payment which thou hast paid us. Blessed be he that shall take and dash thy little ones against the rock.

137

Confitebor tibi

I will praise thee, O LORD, with my whole heart: for thou hast heard the words of my mouth. I will sing praise to thee in the sight of his angels: I will worship towards thy holy temple, and I will give glory to thy name. For thy mercy, and for thy truth: for thou hast magnified thy holy name above all. In what day soever I shall call upon thee, hear me: thou shall multiply strength in my soul. May all the kings of the earth give glory to thee: for they have heard all the words of thy mouth. And let them sing in the ways of the Lord: for great is the glory of the LORD. For the LORD is high, and looketh on the low: and the high he knoweth afar off. If I shall walk in the midst of tribulation, thou wilt quicken me: and thou hast stretched forth thy hand against the wrath of my enemies: and thy right hand hath saved me. The LORD will repay for me: thy mercy, O LORD, endureth forever: O despise not the work of thy hands.

140

Domine, clamavi

I have cried to thee, O LORD, hear me: hearken to my voice, when I cry to thee. Let my prayer be directed as incense in thy sight; the lifting up of my hands, as evening sacrifice. Set a watch, O LORD, before my mouth: and a door round about my lips. Incline not my heart to evil words; to make excuses in sins. With men that work iniquity: and I will not communicate with the choicest of them. The just shall correct me in mercy, and shall reprove me: but let not the oil of the sinner fatten my head. For my prayer also shall still be against the things with which they are well pleased: Their judges falling upon the rock have been swallowed up. They shall hear my words, for they have prevailed: As when the thickness of the earth is broken up upon the ground: Our bones are scattered by the side of hell. But o to thee, O LORD, LORD, are my eyes: in thee have I put my trust, take not away my soul. Keep me from the snare, which they have laid for me, and from the stumbling blocks of them that work iniquity. The wicked shall fall in his net: I am alone until I pass.

141

Voce mea ad Dominum

I cried to the LORD with my voice: with my voice I made supplication to the LORD. In his sight I pour out my prayer, and before him I declare my trouble: When my spirit failed me, then thou knewest my paths. In this way wherein I walked, they have hidden a snare for me. I looked on my right hand, and beheld, and there was no one that would know me. Flight hath failed me: and there is no one that hath regard to my soul. I cried to thee, O LORD: I said: Thou art my hope, my portion in the land of the living. Attend to my supplication: for I am brought very low. Deliver me from my persecutors; for they are stronger than I. Bring my soul out of prison, that I may praise thy name: the just wait for me, until thou reward me.

145

Lauda, anima mea

Praise the LORD, O my soul, in my life I will praise the LORD: I will sing to my God as long as I shall be. Put not your trust in princes: In the children of men, in whom there is no salvation. His spirit shall go forth, and he shall return into his earth: in that day all their thoughts shall perish. Blessed is he who hath the God of Jacob for his helper, whose hope is in the LORD his God: Who made heaven and earth, the sea, and all things that are in them. Who keepeth truth forever: who executeth judgment for them that suffer wrong: who giveth food to the hungry. The LORD looseth them that are fettered: The LORD enlighteneth the blind. The LORD lifteth up them that are cast down: the LORD loveth the just. The LORD keepeth the strangers, he will support the fatherless and the widow: and the ways of sinners he will destroy. The LORD shall reign forever: thy God, O Zion, unto generation and generation.

146

Laudate Dominum

Praise ye the LORD, because psalm is good: to our God be joyful and comely praise. The LORD buildeth up Jerusalem: he will gather together the dispersed of Israel. Who healeth the broken of heart, and bindeth up their bruises. Who telleth the number of the stars: and calleth them all by their names. Great is our LORD, and great is his power: and of his wisdom there is no number. The LORD lifteth up the meek, and bringeth the wicked down even to the ground. Sing ye to the LORD with praise: sing to our God upon the harp. Who covereth the heaven with clouds, and prepareth rain for the earth. Who maketh grass to grow on the mountains, and herbs for the service of men. Who giveth to beasts their food: and to the young ravens that call upon him. He shall not delight in the strength of the horse: nor take pleasure in the legs of a man. The LORD taketh pleasure in them that fear him: and in them that hope in his mercy.

God, make speed to save us. LORD, make haste to help us.

Glory to the Father, and to the Son, and to the Holy Spirit, now and forever, and unto ages of ages. Amen.

A Collect for after the Psalms

God, to whom the heavenly hosts sing,
To whom the saintly church praise,
To whom all spirits worship in song,
Have mercy on all your people,
Who reigns now and ever,
And unto the ages of ages. Amen.

Hymn

Hymn for the Night Vigil

Mediae Noctis Tempus est

Tr. Daniel Joseph Donahoe

The solemn midnight warns us
To heed the prophet's word,
And lift our voice in prayer and praise
To greet our living LORD.
Sing praises to the Father,
Sing praises to the Son,
Sing praises to the Holy Ghost,
The blessed Three in One.
This midnight hour brought terror
To Egypt's land forlorn;
To man and beast death's angel came
And slew the eldest born.
But where the blood was sprinkled
Upon the just man's door,
The angel knew the sacred sign,
And passed that dwelling o'er.

Loud, loud was Egypt's wailing
Beneath the wrath divine;
But Israel sang in psalms of joy,
Protected by the sign.

So we, thy people Israel,
Rejoice, O Lord, in thee;
Saved by the blood of Christ the Lamb,
We spurn the enemy.

And at the hour of midnight,
As by the Gospel shown,
The Bride-groom will in glory come
From Heaven's eternal throne.

And rising up to meet him,
Will the wise Virgins sing,
And lighted by their shining lamps,
Go forth to meet their King.

But they that have been sleeping
Will find, alas, too late,
Their lamps untrimmed, and vainly knock
Against the closed gate.

Let us in sober vigils
Rise up to praise and pray,
And ready be when Jesus comes
To meet him on the way.

At midnight in the prison
Did Paul and Silas see
The shackles burst, while praising Christ,
Who came to set them free.

Out of our worldly prison

We praise thee, Christ our LORD;

O break the bonds of sin for us

Who lean upon thy word,

And grant us, King All-holy,

That we may worthy be

To join with thy celestial choirs

In praise eternally.

A Collect for after the Hymn

Look down, O LORD, at our prayers, you who visits feeble humans, and bestow on us your sanctification and immortality, O Christ, who reigns with the Father and the Holy Spirit, now and ever, and unto the ages of ages. Amen.

Gospel

The Gospel According to St. Matthew

MATTHEW 26:67–75

Then they spat in his face and struck him; and others slapped him, saying, "Prophesy to us, O Christ! Who is it that struck you?" Now Peter sat outside the court and there came to him a servant maid, saying, "You also were with Jesus the Galilean." But he denied it before all of them, saying, "I do not know what you are saying." When he went out of the gate, another maid saw him, and said to the bystanders, "This man was with Jesus of Nazareth." Again he denied with an oath, "I know not the man." After a little while they came that stood by, and said to Peter, "Surely you are also one of them, for even your speech betrays you." Then he began to curse and to swear that he knew not the man. And immediately the cock crowed. Then Peter remembered the word of Jesus which he had said, "Before the cock crows, you will deny me thrice." And going forth, he wept bitterly.

Amen, thanks be to God.

Common Prayer

Remember not the iniquities of our bygone ways and let your mercy come before us quickly, for we have become exceeding poor.

Help us, O God our Savior, for the glory of your name. LORD, deliver us and forgive our sins for your name's sake. Do not give up to the beasts the soul that confesses to you. Forget not the souls of your poor forever. Look upon your covenant, O LORD, who reigns now and ever, and unto the ages of ages. Amen.

For our sins

O God, come to my aid. O LORD, make haste to help me.

Make haste, O LORD, to deliver us from all our sins, who reigns now and ever, and unto the ages of ages. Amen.

For those to be baptized

Save your people, O LORD, and bless your heritage. Rule them and lift them up forever.

Have mercy, O LORD, on your catholic church, which you have redeemed in your holy blood, who reigns now and ever, and unto the ages of ages. Amen.

For the clergy

Arise, O LORD, and go into your eternal peace, you and the ark of your holiness. Your priests will be clothed with justice and your saints exalted.

Let all your saints rejoice in you, O LORD, who places their hope in you in all truth, now and ever, and unto the ages of ages. Amen.

For the people and their leaders

The LORD will give strength to His people; The LORD bless His people in peace.

For the martyrs

By the virtue of your eternal name, Almighty God, we pray you to make us companions of martyrs and of all your saints by the merits of your saints, equal in faith, vigorous in devotion, and like in passion, to make us equal in the resurrection of the fortunate, who reigns now and ever, and unto the ages of ages. Amen.

For the penitents

Have mercy on me, O God, your second great mercy.

Grant us, O LORD, pardon to those who ask you out of faith your second great mercy, O God, who reigns now and ever, and unto the ages of ages. Amen.

Symbol of Faith

We believe in God, the Father almighty, unseen, creator of creatures seen and unseen. We believe in Jesus Christ, His only Son, our LORD, almighty God, conceived by the power of the Holy Spirit, born from the Virgin Mary, suffered under Pontius Pilate; who was crucified, died, and was buried; He descended into Hell; on the third day he rose again from the dead; He ascended into heaven, and is seated at the right hand of God the Father Almighty; from there He will come to judge the living and the dead. We believe in the Holy Spirit, almighty God, of one substance with the Father and Son. The holy catholic church, the forgiveness of sins, communion of saints, and the resurrection of the dead. We believe in life after death, and eternal life in the glory of Christ. All these things we believe in God. Amen.

Divine Prayer

As taught by divine instruction and guided by divine institution, we dare to say:

Our Father in heaven, hallowed be your name; your kingdom come, your will be done, on earth as it is in heaven. Give us today our substantial bread.

Forgive us our debts as we forgive our debtors. Keep us from falling into temptation and deliver us from evil. Amen.

For yours is the kingdom, and the power, and the glory of the Father, and the Son, and Holy Spirit, now and ever, and unto the ages of ages. Amen.

The Order of Nocturn

Invitatory

God, make speed to save us. LORD, make haste to help us.

Glory to the Father, and to the Son, and to the Holy Spirit, now and ever, and unto the ages of ages. Amen.

Hasten, O LORD, to free us from all our sins; for you live and reign with the eternal living Father and the Holy Spirit, now and ever, and unto the ages of ages. Amen.

We have sinned, O LORD, we have sinned, spare us our sins, and save us; you who guided Noah over the flood waves, hear us; who with your word recalled Jonah from the abyss; deliver us; who stretched forth your hand to Peter as he sank, help us, O Christ. Son of God, you accomplished marvelous things of the LORD with our fathers, be favorable in our days also; Stretch forth your hand from on high.

Deliver us, O Christ. Hear us, O Christ. Hear us, O Christ. Hear us, O LORD have mercy.

Son of God, you who did marvelous things of the LORD with our fathers, be favorable in our days also; Stretch forth your hand from on high. Deliver us, O Christ. Hear us, O Christ.

A Collect for the Hour of Nocturn

At midnight hour the angels rejoiced at the birth of our LORD Jesus Christ, and so we ought to rejoice in your peace, Almighty God, who reigns now and ever, and unto the ages of ages. Amen.

Another

Mercifully Jesus, be present with us
With those praying at midnight,
When by divine power
Peter was loosed from his chains;
Who reigns now and ever,
And unto the ages of ages. Amen.

46

Omnes gentes, plaudite

O clap your hands, all ye nations: shout unto God with the voice of Joy, For
the LORD is high, terrible: a great king over all the earth. He hath subdued
the people under us; and the nations under our feet. He hath chosen for us
his inheritance the beauty of Jacob which he hath loved. God is ascended
with jubilee, and the LORD with the sound of trumpet. Sing praises to our
God, sing ye: sing praises to our king, sing ye. For God is the king of all the
earth: sing ye wisely. God shall reign over the nations: God sitteth on his
holy throne. The princes of the people are gathered together, with the God
of Abraham: for the strong gods of the earth are exceedingly exalted.

50

Misere mei, Deus

Have mercy on me, O God, according to thy great mercy. And according to
the multitude of thy tender mercies blot out my iniquity. Wash me yet more
from my iniquity, and cleanse me from my sin. For I know my iniquity, and
my sin is always before me. To thee only have I sinned, and have done evil
before thee: that thou mayst be justified in thy words and mayst overcome
when thou art judged. For behold I was conceived in iniquities; and in sins
did my mother conceive me. For behold thou hast loved truth: the uncertain
and hidden things of thy wisdom thou hast made manifest to me. Thou
shalt sprinkle me with hyssop, and I shall be cleansed: thou shalt wash me,
and I shall be made whiter than snow. To my hearing thou shalt give joy and

gladness: and the bones that have been humbled shall rejoice. Turn away thy face from my sins, and blot out all my iniquities. Create a clean heart in me, O God: and renew a right spirit within my bowels. Cast me not away from thy face; and take not thy holy spirit from me. Restore unto me the joy of thy salvation, and strengthen me with a perfect spirit. I will teach the unjust thy ways: and the wicked shall be converted to thee. Deliver me from blood, O God, thou God of my salvation: and my tongue shall extol thy justice. O LORD, thou wilt open my lips: and my mouth shall declare thy praise. For if thou hadst desired sacrifice, I would indeed have given it: with burnt offerings thou wilt not be delighted. A sacrifice to God is an afflicted spirit: a contrite and humbled heart, O God, thou wilt not despise. Deal favourably, O LORD, in thy good will with Zion; that the walls of Jerusalem may be built up. Then shalt thou accept the sacrifice of justice, oblations and whole burnt offerings: then shall they lay calves upon thy altar.

53

Deus, in nomine

Save me, O God, by thy name, and judge me in thy strength. O God, hear my prayer: give ear to the words of my mouth. For strangers have risen up against me; and the mighty have sought after my soul: and they have not set God before their eyes. For behold God is my helper: and the LORD is the protector of my soul. Turn back the evils upon my enemies; and cut them off in thy truth. I will freely sacrifice to thee, and will give praise, O God, to thy name: because it is good: For thou hast delivered me out of all trouble: and my eye hath looked down upon my enemies.

62

Deus, Deus meus

O God, my God, to thee do I watch at break of day. For thee my soul hath thirsted; for thee my flesh, O how many ways! In a desert land, and where there is no way, and no water: so in the sanctuary have I come before thee, to see thy power and thy glory. For thy mercy is better than lives: thee my lips shall praise. Thus will I bless thee all my life long: and in thy name I will lift up my hands. Let my soul be filled as with marrow and fatness: and my mouth shall praise thee with joyful lips. If I have remembered thee upon my bed, I will meditate on thee in the morning: Because thou hast been my helper. And I will rejoice under the covert of thy wings: My soul hath stuck close to thee: thy right hand hath received me. But they have sought my soul in vain, they shall go into the lower parts of the earth: They shall be delivered into the hands of the sword, they shall be the portions of foxes. But the king shall rejoice in God, all they shall be praised that swear by him: because the mouth is stopped of them that speak wicked things.

66

Deus misereatur

May God have mercy on us, and bless us: may he cause the light of his countenance to shine upon us, and may he have mercy on us. That we may know thy way upon earth: thy salvation in all nations. Let people confess to thee, O God: let all people give praise to thee. Let the nations be glad and rejoice: for thou judgest the people with justice, and directest the nations upon earth. Let the people, O God, confess to thee: let all the people give praise to thee: The earth hath yielded her fruit. May God, our God bless us, May God bless us: and all the ends of the earth fear him.

69

Deus, in adjutorium

O God, come to my assistance; O LORD, make haste to help me. Let them be confounded and ashamed that seek my soul: Let them be turned backward, and blush for shame that desire evils to me: Let them be presently turned away blushing for shame that say to me: Tis well, tis well. Let all that seek thee rejoice and be glad in thee; and let such as love thy salvation say always: The LORD be magnified. But I am needy and poor; O God, help me. Thou art my helper and my deliverer: O LORD, make no delay.

89

Domine, refugium

Before the mountains were made, or the earth and the world was formed; from eternity and to eternity thou art God. Turn not man away to be brought low: and thou hast said: Be converted, O ye sons of men. For a thousand years in thy sight are as yesterday, which is past. And as a watch in the night, Things that are counted nothing, shall their years be. In the morning man shall grow up like grass; in the morning he shall flourish and pass away: in the evening he shall fall, grow dry, and wither. For in thy wrath we have fainted away: and are troubled in thy indignation. Thou hast set our iniquities before thy eyes: our life in the light of thy countenance. For all our days are spent; and in thy wrath we have fainted away. Our years shall be considered as a spider: The days of our years in them are threescore and ten years. But if in the strong they be fourscore years: and what is more of them is labour and sorrow. For mildness is come upon us: and we shall be corrected. Who knoweth the power of thy anger, and for thy fear can number thy wrath? So make thy right hand known: and men learned in heart, in wisdom. Return, O LORD, how long? and be entreated in favour of thy servants. We are filled in the morning with thy mercy: and we have rejoiced, and are delighted all our days. We have rejoiced for the days in which thou hast humbled us: for the years in which we have seen evils. Look upon thy servants and upon their works: and direct their children. And let the brightness of the LORD our God be upon us: and direct thou the works of our hands over us; yea, the work of our hands do thou direct.

114

Dilexi, quoniam

I have loved, because the LORD will hear the voice of my prayer. Because he hath inclined his ear unto me: and in my days I will call upon him. The sorrows of death have encompassed me: and the perils of hell have found me. I met with trouble and sorrow: And I called upon the name of the LORD. O LORD, deliver my soul. The LORD is merciful and just, and our God sheweth mercy. The LORD is the keeper of little ones: I was little and he delivered me. Turn, O my soul, into thy rest: for the LORD hath been bountiful to thee. For he hath delivered my soul from death: my eyes from tears, my feet from falling. I will please the LORD in the land of the living.

115

Credidi, propter quod

I have believed, therefore have I spoken; but I have been humbled exceedingly. I said in my excess: Every man is a liar. What shall I render to the LORD, for all the things he hath rendered unto me? I will take the chalice of salvation; and I will call upon the name of the LORD. I will pay my vows to the LORD before all his people: Precious in the sight of the LORD is the death of his saints. O LORD, for I am thy servant: I am thy servant, and the son of thy handmaid. Thou hast broken my bonds: I will sacrifice to thee the sacrifice of praise, and I will call upon the name of the LORD. I will pay my vows to the LORD in the sight of all his people: In the courts of the house of the LORD, in the midst of thee, O Jerusalem.

119

Ad Dominum

In my trouble I cried to the LORD, and he heard me: "O LORD, deliver my soul from wicked lips, and a deceitful tongue." What shall be given to you? And what shall be added to you, to a deceitful tongue? The sharp arrows of the mighty, with coals that lay waste! Woe is me, that my sojourning is prolonged! I have dwelt with the inhabitants of cedar, that my soul has been long a sojourner. With them that hated peace I was peaceable; but when I spoke to them they fought against me without cause.

120

Levavi oculos

I have lifted up my eyes to the mountains, from whence help shall come to me? My help is from the LORD, who made heaven and earth. May he not suffer your foot to be moved; neither let him slumber that keeps you. Behold he shall neither slumber nor sleep, that keeps Israel. The LORD is your keeper, the LORD is your protection at your right hand. The sun shall not burn you by day, nor the moon by night. The LORD keeps you from all evil; the LORD will keep your soul. The LORD keeps you coming in and you going out from henceforth now and forever.

121

Laetatus sum

I rejoiced at the things that were said to me, "We shall go into the house of the LORD!" Our feet were standing in your courts, O Jerusalem. Jerusalem, built as a city which is compact together. For where the tribes went up, the tribes of the LORD, as was testimony for Israel, to praise the name of the LORD. Because their seats have sat in judgment, seats upon the house of David. Pray for the things that are for the peace of Jerusalem: "May abundance be for them that love you. Let peace be in your strength, and abundance in your towers." For the sake of my brethren, and of my neighbors, I will speak peace of you. Because of the house of the LORD our God, I will seek good things for you.

129

De profundis

Out of the depths I have cried to thee, O LORD: Lord, hear my voice. Let thy ears be attentive to the voice of my supplication. If thou, O LORD, wilt mark iniquities: LORD, who shall stand it. For with thee there is merciful forgiveness: and by reason of thy law, I have waited for thee, O LORD. My soul hath relied on his word: My soul hath hoped in the LORD. From the morning watch even until night, let Israel hope in the LORD. Because with the LORD there is mercy: and with him plentiful redemption. And he shall redeem Israel from all his iniquities.

132

Ecce, quam bonum!

Behold how good and how pleasant it is for brethren to dwell in unity. Like the precious ointment on the head, that ran down upon the beard, the beard of Aaron, Which ran down to the skirt of his garment: As the dew of Hermon, which descendeth upon mount Sion. For there the Lord hath commandeth blessing, and life forevermore.

147

Lauda Jerusalem Dominum

Praise the LORD, O Jerusalem: praise thy God, O Zion. Because he hath strengthened the bolts of thy gates, he hath blessed thy children within thee. Who hath placed peace in thy borders: and filleth thee with the fat of corn. Who sendeth forth his speech to the earth: his word runneth swiftly. Who giveth snow like wool: scattereth mists like ashes. He sendeth his crystal like morsels: who shall stand before the face of his cold? He shall send out his word, and shall melt them: his wind shall blow, and the waters shall run. Who declareth his word to Jacob: his justices and his judgments to Israel. He hath not done in like manner to every nation: and his judgments he hath not made manifest to them. Alleluia.

God, make speed to save us. LORD, make haste to help us.

Glory to the Father, and to the Son, and to the Holy Spirit, now and ever, and unto the ages of ages. Amen.

A Collect for after the Psalms

God, to whom the heavenly hosts sing,
To whom the saintly church praise,
To whom all spirits worship in song,
Have mercy on all your people,
Who reigns, now and ever,
And unto the ages of ages. Amen.

Hymn

Hymn at the Lighting of the Paschal Candle

Ignis Creator

Fiery Creator of fire,

Light Giver of light,

Life Composer of life,

Salvation Giver of deliverance,

The joys of this night,

The watch forsakes the light,

Which is not the power of death,

Enlighten our hearts.

To those departing from Egypt,

Grant your double grace,

Reveal your garment of cloud,

And offer your nocturnal light.

With a column of cloud by day,

You protect the coming people,

With a column of fire at evening,

You dispel the night with light.

Out of the flame, you call forth to your servant

You do not spurn the thorny bush

And though you are a consuming fire,

You do not burn what you illumine.

Embellish the cloudy honeycomb

With all impurities boiled away,

By the fire of the Holy Spirit

The flesh shines like wax.

You now store the hidden comb

The breath of divine honey

Cleansing the innermost heart

Your word has filled the cells.

The swarm of the new youth

Chosen by the Spirit's mouth

Leaving their burdens for heaven

On small wings free from care.

Glory to the Unbegotten Father,

Glory to the Only-begotten,

Together with the Holy Spirit,

For ever and ever.

A Collect for after the Hymn

Look down, O LORD, at our prayers, You who visits feeble humans, and bestow on us your sanctification and immortality, O Christ, who reigns with the eternal living Father and the Holy Spirit, now and ever, and unto the ages of ages. Amen.

Gospel

The Old Testament According to the Book of Exodus

EXODUS 11:1-10

The LORD said to Moses, "I bring one more plague upon Pharaoh and Egypt, and after that he shall let you go and throw you out. Tell all the people that every man ask of his neighbor, and every woman of her neighbour objects of silver and gold." The LORD gave favor to his people in the sight of the Egyptians. Moses was a great man in the land of Egypt, in the sight of Pharaoh's servants, and of all the people. Moses said, "Thus says the LORD: At midnight I will enter into Egypt. Every firstborn in the land of Egypt shall die, from the firstborn of Pharaoh who sits on his throne, even to the firstborn of the female slave behind the handmill, and all the firstborn of beasts. There shall be a loud cry throughout the land of

Egypt, such as never been before, nor shall be hereafter. But with all the children of Israel there a dog shall not growl, not at man or at beast, so that you may know how the difference the LORD makes between Egypt and Israel. Then all these servants of yours shall come down to me, and bow low me, saying, 'Go forth, you and all the people that is under you.' After that we will leave." And exceeding angry he left Pharoah. The LORD said to Moses, "Pharaoh will not listen to you, in order that my signs may be multiplied in the land of Egypt." Moses and Aaron did all the wonders before Pharaoh; but the LORD hardened Pharaoh's heart, and he did not let the children of Israel go out of his land.

Amen, thanks be to God.

The Gospel According to St. Matthew

MATTHEW 25:1-9

"Then the kingdom of heaven be like to ten virgins, who took their lamps and went to meet the bridegroom and the bride. Five of them were foolish, and five wise. But the foolish, having taken their lamps, did not take oil with them; But the wise took oil in their vessels with the lamps. As the bridegroom delayed, they all became drowsy and slept. And at midnight there was a shout, 'Behold! The bridegroom comes! Come out to meet him.' Then all those bridesmaids arose and trimmed their lamps. And the foolish said to the wise, 'Give us some of your oil, for our lamps are going out.' The wise answered, 'There will not be enough for you and for us; go to the dealers and buy for yourselves.' And while they went to buy it, the bridegroom came, and those that were ready went with him to the wedding banquet; and the door was shut. But later came the other bridesmaids, saying, 'LORD, LORD, open to us.' But he replied, 'Amen I tell you, I do not know you.' Keep awake therefore, because you know neither the day nor the hour."

Amen, thanks be to God.

A Collect for after the Gospel

May the spiritual songs and delightful hymns we sing to you, O Christ, please your majesty, as we offer our spiritual sacrifice; you live and reign with the eternal living Father and the Holy Spirit, now and ever, and unto the ages of ages. Amen.

Celebration of Peace

We have acted unjustly, and we have committed iniquities.

You have redeemed us O LORD, God of Truth, by your holy blood now help us in all things Jesus Christ, who lives and reigns with the eternal living Father and the Holy Spirit, now and ever, and unto the ages of ages. Amen.

Great peace to those who love your law, and there is no stumbling block to them.

May your peace O LORD, heavenly king, always remain within us so that we do not fear the night, who lives and reigns with the eternal living Father and the Holy Spirit, now and ever, and unto the ages of ages. Amen.

Symbol of Faith

We believe in God, the Father almighty, unseen, creator of creatures seen and unseen. We believe in Jesus Christ, His only Son, our LORD, almighty God, conceived by the power of the Holy Spirit, born from the Virgin Mary, suffered under Pontius Pilate; who was crucified, died, and was buried; He descended into Hell; on the third day he rose again from the dead; He ascended into heaven, and is seated at the right hand of God the Father Almighty; from there He will come to judge the living and the dead. We believe in the Holy Spirit, almighty God, of one substance with the Father and Son. The holy catholic Church, the forgiveness of sins, communion of saints, and the resurrection of the dead. We believe in life after death, and eternal life in the glory of Christ. All these things we believe in God. Amen.

Divine Prayer

As taught by divine instruction and guided by divine institution, we dare to say:

Our Father in heaven, hallowed be your name; your kingdom come, your will be done, on earth as it is in heaven. Give us today our substantial bread. Forgive us our debts as we forgive our debtors. Keep us from falling into temptation and deliver us from evil. Amen.

For yours is the kingdom, and the power, and the glory of the Father, and the Son, and Holy Spirit, now and ever, and unto the ages of ages. Amen.

Canticles

Audite coeli

Deuteronomy 32:1–42

Hear, O ye heavens, the things I speak, let the earth give ear to the words of my mouth.

Let my doctrine gather as the rain, let my speech distil as the dew, as a shower upon the herb, and as drops upon the grass.

Because I will invoke the name of the Lord: give ye magnificence to our God.

The works of God are perfect, and all his ways are judgments: God is faithful and without any iniquity, he is just and right.

They have sinned against him, and are nose of his children in their filth: they are a wicked and perverse generation.

Is this the return thou makest to the LORD, O foolish and senseless people? Is not he thy father, that hath possessed thee, and made thee, and created thee?

Remember the days of old, think upon every generation: ask thy father, and he will declare to thee: thy elders and they will tell thee.

When the Most High divided the nations: when he separated the sons of Adam, he appointed the bounds of people according to the number of the children of Israel.

But the LORD's portion is his people: Jacob the lot of his inheritance.

He found him in a desert land, in a place of horror, and of vast wilderness: he led him about, and taught him: and he kept him as the apple of his eye.

As the eagle enticing her young to fly, and hovering over them, he spread his wings, and hath taken him and carried him on his shoulders.

The LORD alone was his leader: and there was no strange god with him.

He set him upon high land: that he might eat the fruits of the fields, that he might suck honey out of the rock, and oil out of the hardest stone,

Butter of the herd, and milk of the sheep with the fat of lambs, and of the rams of the breed of Basan: and goats with the marrow of wheat, and might drink the purest blood of the grape.

The beloved grew fat, and kicked: he grew fat, and thick and gross, he forsook God who made him, and departed from God his saviour.

They provoked him by strange gods, and stirred him up to anger, with their abominations.

They sacrificed to devils and not to God: to gods whom they knew not: that were newly come up, whom their fathers worshipped not.

Thou hast forsaken the God that beget thee, and hast forgotten the LORD that created thee.

The LORD saw, and was moved to wrath: because his own sons and daughters provoked him.

And he said: I will hide my face from them, and will consider what their last end shall be: for it is a perverse generation, and unfaithful children.

They have provoked me with that which was no god, and have angered me with their vanities: and I will provoke them with that which is no people, and will vex them with a foolish nation.

A fire is kindled in my wrath, and shall burn even to the lowest hell: and shall devour the earth with her increase, and shall burn the foundations of the mountains.

I will heap evils upon them, and will spend my arrows among them.

They shall be consumed with famine, and birds shall devour them with a most bitter bite: I will send the teeth of beasts upon them, with the fury of creatures that trail upon the ground, and of serpents.

Without, the sword shall lay them waste, and terror within, both the young man and the virgin, the sucking child with the man in years.

I said: Where are they? I will make the memory of them to cease from among men.

But for the wrath of the enemies I have deferred it: lest perhaps their enemies might be proud, and should say: Our mighty hand, and not the LORD, hath done all these things.

They are a nation without counsel, and without wisdom.

O that they would be wise and would understand, and would provide for their last end.

How should one pursue after a thousand, and two chase ten thousand? Was it not, because their God had sold them, and the Lord had shut them up?

For our God is not as their gods: our enemies themselves are judges.

Their vines are of the vineyard of Sodom, and of the suburbs of Gomorrha: their grapes are grapes of gall, and their clusters most bitter.

Their wine is the gall of dragons, and the venom of asps, which is incurable.

Are not these things stored up with me, and sealed up in my treasures?

Revenge is mine, and I will repay them in due time, that their foot may slide: the day of destruction is at hand, and the time makes haste to come.

The LORD will judge his people, and will have mercy on his servants: he shall see that their hand is weakened, and that they who were shut up have also failed, and they that remained are consumed.

And he shall say: Where are their gods, in whom they trusted?

Of whose victims they ate the fat, and drank the wine of their drink offerings: let them arise and help you, and protect you in your distress.

See ye that I alone am, and there is no other God besides me: I will kill and I will make to live: I will strike, and I will heal, and there is none that can deliver out of my hand.

I will lift up my hand to heaven, and I will say: I live forever.

If I shall whet my sword as the lightning, and my hand take hold on judgment: I will render vengeance to my enemies, and repay them that hate me.

I will make my arrows drunk with blood, and my sword shall devour flesh, of the blood of the slain and of the captivity, of the bare head of the enemies.

Benedictus

Luke 1:68–79

Blessed be the LORD God of Israel; because he hath visited and wrought the redemption of his people:

And hath raised up an horn of salvation to us, in the house of David his servant:

As he spoke by the mouth of his holy prophets, who are from the beginning:

Salvation from our enemies, and from the hand of all that hate us:

To perform mercy to our fathers, and to remember his holy testament,

The oath, which he swore to Abraham our father, that he would grant to us,

That being delivered from the hand of our enemies, we may serve him without fear,

In holiness and justice before him, all our days.

And thou, child, shalt be called the prophet of the Highest: for thou shalt go before the face of the LORD to prepare his ways:

To give knowledge of salvation to his people, unto the remission of their sins:

Through the bowels of the mercy of our God, in which the Orient from on high hath visited us:

To enlighten them that sit in darkness, and in the shadow of death: to direct our feet into the way of peace.

Cantemus Domino

Exodus 15:1–6, 11–13, 17–18

Let us sing to the LORD: for he is gloriously magnified, the horse and the rider he hath thrown into the sea.

The LORD is my strength and my praise, and he is become salvation to me: he is my God and I will glorify him: the God of my father, and I will exalt him.

The LORD is as a man of war, Almighty is his name.

Pharao's chariots and his army he hath cast into the sea: his chosen captains are drowned in the Red Sea.

The depths have covered them, they are sunk to the bottom like a stone.

Thy right hand, O LORD, is magnified in strength: thy right hand, O LORD, hath slain the enemy.

Who is like to thee, among the strong, O LORD? who is like to thee, glorious in holiness, terrible and praiseworthy, doing wonders?

Thou stretchedst forth thy hand, and the earth swallowed them.

In thy mercy thou hast been a leader to the people which thou hast redeemed: and in thy strength thou hast carried them to thy holy habitation.

Thou shalt bring them in, and plant them in the mountain of thy inheritance, in thy most firm habitation which thou hast made, O Lord; thy sanctuary, O LORD, which thy hands have established.

The LORD shall reign forever and ever.

Benedicite

Song of the Three Young Men, 35–65

O all ye Works of the LORD, bless ye the LORD: praise him, and magnify him forever.

O ye Angels of the LORD, bless ye the LORD: praise him, and magnify him forever.

O ye Heavens, bless ye the LORD: praise him, and magnify him forever.

O ye Waters that be above the Firmament, bless ye the LORD: praise him, and magnify him forever.

O all ye Powers of the LORD, bless ye the LORD: praise him, and magnify him forever.

O ye Sun and Moon, bless ye the LORD: praise him, and magnify him forever.

O ye Stars of Heaven, bless ye the LORD: praise him, and magnify him forever.

O ye Showers and Dew, bless ye the LORD: praise him, and magnify him forever.

O ye Winds of God, bless ye the LORD: praise him, and magnify him forever.

O ye Fire and Heat, bless ye the LORD: praise him, and magnify him forever.

O ye Winter and Summer, bless ye the LORD: praise him, and magnify him forever.

O ye Dews and Frosts, bless ye the LORD: praise him, and magnify him forever.

O ye Frost and Cold, bless ye the LORD: praise him, and magnify him forever.

O ye Ice and Snow, bless ye the LORD: praise him, and magnify him forever.

O ye Nights and Days, bless ye the LORD: praise him, and magnify him forever.

O ye Light and Darkness, bless ye the LORD: praise him, and magnify him forever.

O ye Lightnings and Clouds, bless ye the LORD: praise him, and magnify
    him forever.

O let the Earth bless the LORD: yea, let it praise him, and magnify
    him forever.

O ye Mountains and Hills, bless ye the LORD: praise him, and magnify
    him forever.

O all ye Green Things upon the Earth, bless ye the LORD: praise him,
    and magnify him forever.

O ye Wells, bless ye the LORD: praise him, and magnify him forever.

O ye Seas and Floods, bless ye the LORD: praise him, and magnify
    him forever.

O ye Whales, and all that move in the Waters, bless ye the LORD: praise
    him, and magnify him forever.

O all ye Fowls of the Air, bless ye the LORD: praise him, and magnify
    him forever.

O all ye Beasts and Cattle, bless ye the LORD: praise him, and magnify
    him forever.

O ye Children of Men, bless ye the LORD: praise him, and magnify
    him forever.

O let Israel bless the LORD: praise him and magnify him forever.

O ye Priests of the LORD, bless ye the LORD: praise him, and magnify
    him forever.

O ye Servants of the LORD, bless ye the LORD: praise him, and magnify
    him forever.

O ye Spirits and Souls of the Righteous, bless ye the LORD: praise him,
    and magnify him forever.

O ye holy and humble Men of heart, bless ye the LORD: praise him,
    and magnify him forever.

Hymns

Let the Band of Brothers Sing a Hymn

Hymnum dicat turba fratrum

TR. DANIEL JOSEPH DONAHOE, 1911

Raise the song, O band of brothers,
Let the holy anthem ring;
Sound the hymn of loud laudation,
Unto Christ, our LORD and King.
Gentle Jesus, hear our voices:
Thee the Word, the Truth, the Way,
Rod of Jesse, Judah's Lion;
Thee we praise, to thee we pray.
At the right hand of the Father
Is thy throne, Most Holy One,
Thou, our Lamb, our Mount of Refuge,
Rock of hope and Corner Stone.
LORD, we hail thee as the Bride-groom,
As our Light, our Heavenly Door;
Dove of peace and tender Shepherd,
Be our guide forevermore.
By the voice of bard and prophet,
Was thy holy birth foretold,

Ere the star of morn begotten;
Maker of the world of old.
Maker of the earth and heaven,
Thou of all art LORD and King
Who didst gather up the waters
And the stars from darkness bring.
Through the womb of spotless Virgin
Thou as Saviour of the earth
Camest when the angel's "Ave"
Heralded by wondrous birth.
Lo, thy star the Magi follow,
And their Orient offerings bring,
Bowing down in adoration
To the Child as LORD and King.
Envious Herod hears and trembles
And he seeks the babe to slay,
Sheds the blood of infant martyrs,
But the Christ is borne away.
By an angel warned, the mother,
To the country of the Nile
Bears the blessed Child in safety,
And escapes the tyrant's guile.
Here as wanderers they tarry
Till the cruel monarch's death;
Then to Galilee returning
Seek their home at Nazareth.
Here in youth and early manhood
Many wondrous works were done;
Heavenly blessing for his people

Wrought the Christ, our Holy One.

And he preached the heavenly Kingdom,

Proving by his work the word;

Healed the sick, the blind illumined,

And the dead to life restored.

At the wedding feast of Cana

Was the water changed to wine;

With the loaves and fish, he furnished

For the throngs, a feast divine.

From his followers were chosen

Twelve to preach the living word;

One of these, the traitor Judas,

By a kiss betrayed the Lord.

Then came messengers from Annas,

Seized the Christ and led Him bound

Unto Pilate's hall for judgment,

Who in him no evil found.

But his life the mob demanded

As a foe of Caesar's throne;

So the governor delivered

To their hands the Holy One.

Then they scorned and scourged the Saviour,

Crowned with thorns and crucified;

Led him as a lamb to slaughter,

And to conquer death he died.

When he yielded up the spirit

Daylight fled and quaked the earth;

Then the temple veil was rended,

And from graves the dead came forth.

Now at eve the blessed Joseph
Lays the body in the tomb,
Where a guard of Roman Soldiers
At the priests' request is come.
While they watch the tomb, an angel,
Robed in white like morning's ray,
They behold with trembling terror,
As he rolls the stone away.
And they see the Christ triumphant
From the broken tomb arise,
This the impious Jew beholdeth,
This the impious Jew denies.
First unto the weeping woman
Doth the risen LORD appear,
Changing unto joy their sorrows,
While his gentle voice they hear.
Then unto the twelve he cometh,
Greeteth them with grace benign,
Fills them with the Holy Spirit,
Teaching them the law divine;
Send them forth to preach his gospel,
And his witnesses to be;
Bids them to baptize the nations
In the Blessed Trinity.
Ere the ray of morning riseth,
Band of brothers, raise the song,
Send the truth to future ages;
Honor, praise, and love prolong.
While the bird or morn, awaking,

Sings aloud and beats his wing,

And the light of day appeareth,

Let our hearts with gladness ring.

Sing the glory of the Saviour,

Sing his mighty Majesty;

Gentle Christ, our Lord and ruler,

Keep our hearts on high with thee.

Come all ye holy

Sancti venite

TR. JOHN MASON NEALE, 1851

Draw nigh and take the Body of the LORD,

and drink the holy Blood for you outpoured.

Saved by that Body and that precious Blood,

with souls refreshed, we render thanks to God.

Salvation's Giver, Christ, the only Son,

by his dear Cross and Blood the victory won.

Offered was he for greatest and for least,

himself the Victim, and himself the Priest.

Victims were offered by the law of old,

which in a type this heavenly mystery foretold.

He, Ransomer, from death, and Light from shade,

now gives his holy grace his saints to aid;

approach ye then with faithful hearts sincere,

and take the safeguard of salvation here.

He that in this world rules his saints and shields,

to all believers life eternal yields.

With heavenly bread makes them that hunger whole,

gives living waters to the thirsting soul.

Alpha and Omega, to whom shall bow

all nations at the Doom, is with us now.

Hymn at the Lighting of the Paschal Candle

Ignis Creator

Fiery Creator of fire,

Light Giver of light,

Life Composer of life,

Salvation Giver of deliverance,

The joys of this night,

The watch forsakes the light,

Which is not the power of death,

Enlighten our hearts.

To those departing from Egypt,

Grant your double grace,

Reveal your garment of cloud,

And offer your nocturnal light.

With a column of cloud by day,

You protect the coming people,

With a column of fire at evening,

You dispel the night with light.

Out of the flame, you call forth to your servant

You do not spurn the thorny bush

And though you are a consuming fire,

You do not burn what you illumine.

Embellish the cloudy honeycomb

With all impurities boiled away,

By the fire of the Holy Spirit
The flesh shines like wax.
You now store the hidden comb
The breath of divine honey
Cleansing the innermost heart
Your word has filled the cells.
The swarm of the new youth
Chosen by the Spirit's mouth
Leaving their burdens for heaven
On small wings free from care.
Glory to the Unbegotten Father,
Glory to the Only-begotten,
Together with the Holy Spirit,
For ever and ever.

Hymn for the Night Vigil

Mediae Noctis Tempus est

Tr. Daniel Joseph Donahoe

The solemn midnight warns us
To heed the prophet's word,
And lift our voice in prayer and praise
To greet our living LORD.
Sing praises to the Father,
Sing praises to the Son,
Sing praises to the Holy Ghost,
The blessed Three in One.
This midnight hour brought terror
To Egypt's land forlorn;

To man and beast death's angel came

And slew the eldest born.

But where the blood was sprinkled

Upon the just man's door,

The angel knew the sacred sign,

And passed that dwelling o'er.

Loud, loud was Egypt's wailing

Beneath the wrath divine;

But Israel sang in psalms of joy,

Protected by the sign.

So we, thy people Israel,

Rejoice, O LORD, in thee;

Saved by the blood of Christ the Lamb,

We spurn the enemy.

And at the hour of midnight,

As by the Gospel shown,

The Bride-groom will in glory come

From Heaven's eternal throne.

And rising up to meet him,

Will the wise Virgins sing,

And lighted by their shining lamps,

Go forth to meet their King.

But they that have been sleeping

Will find, alas, too late,

Their lamps untrimmed, and vainly knock

Against the closed gate.

Let us in sober vigils

Rise up to praise and pray,

And ready be when Jesus comes

To meet him on the way.

At midnight in the prison

Did Paul and Silas see

The shackles burst, while praising Christ,

Who came to set them free.

Out of our worldly prison

We praise thee, Christ our LORD;

O break the bonds of sin for us

Who lean upon thy word,

And grant us, King All-holy,

That we may worthy be

To join with thy celestial choirs

In praise eternally.

Martyrs of the God Most High

Sacratissimi Martyres

TR. WILLIAM GARDEN BLAIKIE

Martyrs of the God Most High,

Who for Christ did bravely die;

Leaders on the heavenly road;

Victors, sing with saints to God, Alleluia!

Christ exalted! Cherubim

Render homage unto Him

On the Father's throne on high,

While the saints with martyrs cry, Alleluia!

Glorious One! The first to bear

Shame upon the Cross, our share;

In Thy triumph blessing came;

Now the martyr saints proclaim, Alleluia!

The Apostles, strong in faith,

Suffered on the Cross to death;

Shielded now, and saved by grace,

Chant within Thy holy place, Alleluia!

Christ! The Helper of the saints,

Heard their weary hearts' complaints;

Now these martyrs praises bring

And rehearse before their King, Alleluia!

Praised, O LORD, Thy power be,

Which obtains the victory;

Crushes Satan by the way,

While the saints with martyrs say, Alleluia!

God's strong hand will be their shield;

With His grace their hearts are steeled

To resist the enemy's ways,

While with saints they ever raise, Alleluia.

Heirs with Christ! Their crowns behold!

Filled with fruit a hundred-fold!

Pains are past; they now rejoice,

Uttering in thankful voice, Alleluia.

Saint Sechnall's Hymn to Saint Patrick

Audite omnes amantes

Tr. Fr. Atkinson, S.J.

Listen ye lovers of God as I tell you of Patrick the Bishop,

Man whom the Master hath blest, hero of saintly deserts;

How for the good that he does upon earth, he is likened to angels,

How for his life without flaw, peer of Apostles he stands.

Every tittle he guards of the mandates of Christ the All-Blessed;

Bright in the sight of the world glitters the light of his works;

Wondrous and holy indeed the example he sets and men follow,

Praising the LORD for it all, praising the Father above.

Steadfast is he in the fear of his Maker; his faith is unshaken;

Firm as on Peter the Church rises up-builded on him;

God hath allotted to him the place of Apostle within it,

'Gainst it the portals of hell never are strong to prevail.

Him hath the Master elected a teacher of barbarous races,

Cunning with seine of the truth, fishing for men with his net,

So that from waves of the world he may win unto grace the believing,

Making them follow their LORD up to his throne in the skies.

Christ's are the talents he sells, the excellent coin of good tidings,

Claiming them back from our clans, fruitful with usury's gain;

Certain for meed of his toil, for price of his prodigal labour,

Some day with Christ to possess joy in his heavenly realm.

Faithful in service to God is he God's most glorious envoy,

Model and type to the good what an Apostle should be,

Preacher with word and with action to such as God calls for his people,

So that if word be too weak, action may urge them to good.

Christ hath his glory in keeping, yet here upon earth is he honoured,

Worshipped by all who behold, e'en as an angel of God;

Yea, for as Paul to the Gentiles, so God hath sent him his Apostle,

Guiding the steps of men home, unto the Kingdom of God.

Humble in spirit and body, the fear of his Maker hath filled him,

Though for his goodness the Lord loveth to rest on his soul;

Deep in his flesh that is sinless he carries the mark of the Master,

Patiently bearing nor e'er glorying save in the Cross.

Dauntless and restless he feeds the believing with heavenly banquets,

Lest they that journey with Christ, faint as they walk on the road,

Furnishing forth unto all for their bread the words of the Gospel

Lo! as the manna of old multiplied still in his hands.

Chaste for the love of his Lord, he warily keepeth his body

Wrought and adorned as a shrine, meet for the Spirit of God:

Yea, and the Spirit for ever abides amid works that are cleanly,

Yea, 'tis a victim he gives living and pleasing to God.

Light of the world is he, kindled ablaze, as was told in the Gospel,

Lighted and set on the stand, shining far out to mankind:

Stronghold is he of the King, a city placed high on the hill-top

Plentiful riches are there, stored for the Master of all.

Surely shall Patrick be called in the heavenly kingdom the greatest,

Who what his holy words teach, bodies in goodness of deed;

Pattern and model of all, he guides the van of the faithful,

Keeping in pureness of heart trust ever clinging to God.

Boldly he blazons the name of the LORD to the infidel races,

Giving them grace without end, out of the laver of life.

Day after day for their sins unto God he makes his petition,

Slaying for health of their souls victims worthy of God.

Worldly acclaim doth he flout, that God's law may yet be established,

While at God's Table he stands, all is as dross in his eyes;

Thunder of this world may crash; undaunted he faces its crashing,

Glad in the tempest of wrong, since that he suffers for Christ.

Shepherd so faithful and true of the flock that the Gospel has won him,

Chosen by God's own self ward of the people of God,

Chosen to pasture His people with teaching appointed from heaven,

Risking his life for the flock, after the pattern of Christ.

Him hath the Saviour raised to be Bishop because of his merits,

Counsellor unto the priests fighting the battle of God,

Giving them raiment to wear and food from a heavenly storehouse,

Holy celestial words, quitting his task to the full.

Lo! to the faithful he bears the call of the King to his nuptials,

Wearing the nuptial robe, clad with the garment of grace.

Heavenly wine doth he draw without stint in celestial vessels,

Bidding God's people approach unto the heavenly cup.

Hid in the sacred Books, a sacred treasure he found him,

Seeing the Godhead clear under the Saviour's Flesh,

Holy and all complete are his merits that purchase the treasure.

'Warrior of God,' is he called, looking on God with his soul.

Faithful witness is he of the LORD in catholic precepts,

Precepts carefully stored, salt with the message divine;

So that man's flesh may never corrupt into food for the earth-worms,

Kept by the heavenly juice fresh to be offered to God.

Labourer noble and loyal is he in the field of the Gospel,

Sowing in sight of the world seeds of good tidings of Christ;

Sowing with lips that God guards seed in the ears of the wary,

Making their hearts and their minds tilth of the Spirit of God.

Christ for Himself hath made choice; his deputy here hath he placed him,

Out of two tyrants' holds setting their prisoners free

Ransoming slaves from the chains of men who held them in bondage,

Freeing from Satan's rule numberless souls that were his.

Hymns and psalms doth he sing to the LORD with St. John's Revelations;

Chanting to hasten his work, building the people of God.

Into their keeping he gives the law in the Name of the Triune,

Teaching the Persons are Three, simple the Substance of God.

Girt with the girdle of God, by day and by night never ceasing

Unto his Lord and his God, riseth his prayer without rest;

Mighty the toil is, and sure the guerdon that waits for his labour

Lordship along with the Twelve over the people of God.

Listen ye lovers of God as I tell you of Patrick the Bishop,

Man whom the Master hath blest, hero of saintly deserts;

How for the good that he does upon earth, he is likened to angels

How for his life without flaw, peer of Apostles he stands.

Glory Be to God

Gloria in Excelsis Deo

FROM THE BOOK OF COMMON PRAYER, 1892

Glory be to God on high

And in earth peace, goodwill towards men,

We praise thee, we bless thee,

we worship thee, we glorify thee,

we give thanks to thee, for thy great glory

O LORD God, heavenly King,

God the Father Almighty.

O LORD, the only-begotten Son, Jesu Christ;

O LORD God, Lamb of God, Son of the Father,

that takest away the sins of the world,

have mercy upon us.

Thou that takest away the sins of the world,

have mercy upon us.

Thou that takest away the sins of the world,

receive our prayer.

Thou that sittest at the right hand of God the Father,

have mercy upon us.

For thou only art holy;

thou only art the Lord;

thou only, O Christ,

with the Holy Ghost,

art most high

in the glory of God the Father. Amen.

Thee, O God, we praise

Te Deum laudamus

FROM THE BOOK OF COMMON PRAYER, 1892

We praise thee, O God: we acknowledge thee to be the LORD.

All the earth doth worship thee: the Father everlasting.

To thee all Angels cry aloud: the Heavens, and all the Powers therein.

To thee Cherubim and Seraphim: continually do cry,

Holy, Holy, Holy: LORD God of Sabaoth;

Heaven and earth are full of the Majesty: of thy glory.

The glorious company of the Apostles: praise thee.

The goodly fellowship of the Prophets: praise thee.

The noble army of Martyrs: praise thee.

The holy Church throughout all the world : doth acknowledge thee;

The Father: of an infinite Majesty;

Thine honourable, true: and only Son;

Also the Holy Ghost: the Comforter.

Thou art the King of Glory: O Christ.

Thou art the everlasting Son: of the Father.

When thou tookest upon thee to deliver man: thou didst not abhor
the Virgin's womb.

When thou hadst overcome the sharpness of death: thou didst open the
Kingdom of Heaven to all believers.

Thou sittest at the right hand of God: in the glory of the Father.

We believe that thou shalt come: to be our Judge.

We therefore pray thee, help thy servants: whom thou hast redeemed with thy precious blood.

Make them to be numbered with thy Saints: in glory everlasting.

O LORD, save thy people: and bless thine heritage.

Govern them: and lift them up forever.

Day by day: we magnify thee;

And we worship thy Name: ever world without end.

Vouchsafe, O LORD: to keep us this day without sin.

O LORD, have mercy upon us: have mercy upon us.

O LORD, let thy mercy lighten upon us: as our trust is in thee.

O LORD, in thee have I trusted: let me never be confounded.

Bibliography

Jeffery, Peter. "Eastern and Western Elements in the Irish Monastic Prayer of the Hours." In *The Divine Office in the Latin Middle Ages: Methodology and Source Studies, Regional Developments, Hagiography*, edited by Margot E. Fassler and Rebecca A. Baltzer. New York: Oxford University Press, 2000.

Kardong, Terrence G. *St. Columban: His Life, Rule, Legacy*. Collegeville: Liturgical, 2017.

McNamara, Martin J. "*Navigatio sancti Brendani*: Some Possible Connections with Liturgical, Apocryphal, and Irish Tradition." In *The Brendan Legend: Text and Versions*, edited by Glen S. Burgess and Clara Strijbosch. Boston: Brill, 2006.

McNamara, Martin J. *Psalms in the Early Irish Church*. Sheffield: Sheffield Academic Press, 2000.

O'Laughlin, Thomas. "The Monastic Liturgy of the Hours in the *Nauigatio sancti Brendani*: A Preliminary Investigation." *Irish Theological Quarterly* 71, (2006): 113–126.

Warren, F. E., ed. *The Antiphonary of Bangor: An Early Irish Manuscript in the Ambrosian Library at Milan*. London: Harrison and Sons, 1895.